AHEAD OF TIME

20 Leading Minds Shaping the Future

Table of Contents

9	**Sam Altman** Founder of OpenAI	AI TECHNOLOGY
17	**Spencer Bailey** Founder of The Slowdown	MEDIA
29	**Jonathan Berte** Chairman and Founder of Robovision	AI TECHNOLOGY
41	**Luca de Meo** Chief Executive Officer at Kering	LUXURY
53	**Marcus Engman** Chief Creative Officer at IKEA Retail	DESIGN
65	**Tony Fadell** Founder of Build Collective	TECHNOLOGY
79	**Tina Fordham** Geopolitical Strategist and Founder of Fordham Global Foresight	GEOPOLITICS
91	**Joe Gebbia** Co-Founder of Airbnb and Samara	TECHNOLOGY
101	**Lonneke Gordijn** Co-Founder of Studio DRIFT	ART
111	**Christopher D. Harvey** Professor of Neurobiology at Harvard Medical School	SCIENCE

123	*Masayuki Hirota* Editor-in-Chief at Chronos Japan	MEDIA
135	*John Jay* President of Global Creative at Fast Retailing	FASHION
147	*Tiina Karjalainen Kierysch* Head of Design at Bang & Olufsen	DESIGN
157	*Daniel Libeskind* Founder of Studio Libeskind	ARCHITECTURE
167	*Virgilio Martínez* Chef and Restaurateur	HOSPITALITY
179	*Garry Nolan* Professor at Stanford University	SCIENCE
195	*Ivy Ross* Chief Design Officer for Consumer Devices at Google	TECHNOLOGY
207	*Stefan Sagmeister* Founder of Sagmeister Inc.	DESIGN
219	*Phil Schiller* Apple Fellow	TECHNOLOGY
229	*Tom Segura* Stand-up Comedian and Writer	ENTERTAINMENT

Fore word

The future offers more than the past. This belief lives at the heart of everything we do at Ressence, connecting our watchmaking brand to the talent you'll meet in the pages ahead.

When I founded Ressence in 2010, I consciously chose to break with tradition. As an industrial designer and outsider, I saw an industry consistently referencing the past. We moved in the opposite direction, embracing the future and freeing ourselves from watchmaking's obsession with what I call 'reorganising the museum'. This allowed us to apply contemporary logic and twenty-first-century design thinking to our products. Fifteen years later, in 2025, and with a rich catalogue of innovative designs behind us, it's clear this approach has paid off. To mark this moment, we've commissioned a book celebrating fifteen years of our forward-looking philosophy – but more importantly, highlighting people who share our future-positive mindset.

In the following pages, you'll discover architects reimagining human experience, designers channelling optimism into technology's potential for good, and entrepreneurs balancing progress with positive impact – all with a forward-thinking attitude. These essential voices are visionaries reshaping industries by keeping their eyes firmly on the future.

Ahead of their time, our twenty interviewees achieved success by seeing something others didn't. They saw potential in what was to come. Their conversations reveal a common theme – an unwavering belief that tomorrow can be better than today. Unsurprisingly, most of our interviewees are entrepreneurs or highly entrepreneurially minded. As someone who built a business from scratch, I admire their journeys and the mindset behind their success. Entrepreneurs possess brave energy, betting astutely on their strengths and spotting demand before others recognise the supply.

Most importantly, the best entrepreneurs remain humble despite extraordinary success. This humility, paired with curiosity and optimism, forms the foundation of genuine innovation. The talent featured in *Ahead of Time* meets these criteria. They practise their craft at the top of their disciplines with inspiring openness. It's this openness I want to thank them for – for sharing their views on where their industries, and humanity as a whole, are heading with us.

For you, dear reader, I hope you approach this book with an open mind. As we age, we sometimes allow the never-easy past to darken our view of the future. Instead, I encourage you to consume this content with childlike curiosity. Children are naturally curious, not cynical or pessimistic, without an 'I've seen it all' mentality. They're eager to discover new ideas, find fresh ways of doing things, and remain optimistic about innovation. The people in this book maintain that childlike wonder while shaping the future, and I hope this book will bring a little more wonder into your life.

This book isn't about watchmaking – it's about mindset. It's about believing that creativity, innovation, and human ingenuity will always create more value than wallowing in nostalgia. It's about having the courage to take risks, to be ahead of time, and to build something better.

The future is uncertain, but that's precisely what makes it exciting.

Benoît Mintiens
Founder of RESSENCE

Sam Altman

As CEO of OpenAI, Altman has propelled generative tools like ChatGPT into the mainstream. Simultaneously he has pioneered the clean energy industry through ventures such as nuclear fusion startup Helion Energy. His dual focus makes him uniquely positioned to shape a future abundant in both intelligence and sustainable energy.

FOUNDER OF OPENAI

Sam Altman occupies a rare vantage point at the intersection of artificial intelligence and clean energy – two spheres poised to reshape society dramatically in the years ahead. As CEO of OpenAI, he has accelerated breakthroughs in artificial intelligence, making powerful tools like ChatGPT widely accessible. Concurrently, Altman champions clean energy innovation through strategic investments, including nuclear fusion at Helion Energy, where he serves as executive chairman. He also advanced nuclear fission via another startup, Oklo. These ambitious ventures reflect his belief that abundant, sustainable energy is the essential infrastructure for the AI-driven world that lies ahead.

This dual commitment embodies Altman's clear-eyed optimism. He identifies intelligence and energy as foundational to human advancement, viewing their potential abundance as a gateway to global prosperity and improved quality of life. Altman envisions a near future where medical care, education, and essential resources become radically more affordable, reshaping economic structures in ways not seen for generations. Yet he remains pragmatic about this significant change's ability to make societies even more uneven. With this in mind, he emphasises that embracing abundance demands careful consideration and responsible governance.

Altman, however, doesn't believe a brand new AI-enhanced future will be too confronting for most of us. "I believe deeply in humanity's adaptability", he asserts, but he notes that vigilance must accompany optimism. This thoughtful approach underscores his philosophy: technology is neither inherently good nor bad, but a reflection of our intentions and oversight.

His business leadership approach aligns with these views, grounded in consistent and daily encouragement rather than singular dramatic gestures. Altman describes fostering innovation at OpenAI through steady inspiration, urging teams to take thoughtful risks and think expansively at every opportunity. When Ahead of Time visited the brand's headquarters in San Francisco, we learnt that Altman had republished Arthur C. Clarke's visionary classic *Profiles of the Future* for his team – a book that presciently explores humanity's potential through technological innovation. Like Clarke, Altman perceives human potential as boundless, provided the proper resources and moral compass are in place. Altman, therefore, presents a future horizon worth aiming for: one defined by innovation, informed by vigilance, and ultimately enriched by humanity.

Recently becoming a father has deepened Altman's reflections on the long-term implications of technology. He recognises his child will never experience a world untouched by intelligent machines, making the stakes personal and immediate. Rather than viewing this inevitability with trepidation, Altman remains optimistic. He sees intelligent machines not as threats, but as indispensable tools for a generation more capable and empowered than any that has come before.

What technological advancements are you most excited by?

So, first of all, intelligence and energy are the two fundamental inputs. With good ideas and the ability to move and manipulate matter, we can do everything else. In a sense, the most significant developments currently underway are the increasing abundance of energy and intelligence. Throughout my career, driving towards these abundances has been my two biggest missions. However, I didn't know how directly they would come together. I didn't realise that the price of intelligence would eventually converge with the price of energy. It now appears pretty obvious that this is happening. With these two factors being key to economic growth and improving the quality of human life, nations that are enabled to remove constraints on them are likely to enjoy a massive impact.

And what will a world where intelligence and energy are much more abundant look like?

If you can relax the constraints on intelligence and energy, I don't think we fully understand yet what that world will look like. However, I'm very excited to find out. It will be a world of great abundance. It'll be a little uneven, maybe houses stay expensive, but maybe medical care gets really cheap, or something like that. It feels like the most significant reshuffle of our economy in a long time.

Why did you choose to focus on energy so early in your career, and why does it remain important for you with your investments in operations like Helion Energy?

I remember learning in school that the single biggest contributor to the increase in quality of life over time was a decrease in the cost of energy. And it made total sense to me. My mindset was: we should push that much further. And I began thinking about how we can push this as far as possible.

How do you separate visionary foresight from flawed forecasting?

==When the stakes are very high, you try to rely more on forecasting. Once the stakes are lower, you can rely more on vision and intuition.== So if you're going to spend ten billion dollars on one training run, you'd like to believe it's going to work. If you're going to spend ten million, you can take more of a flyer.

How has having a child affected the way that you think about deep philosophical questions regarding consciousness, relating to both human beings and AI?

In some ways, having a baby feels like the most normal thing I've ever done, and in other ways, it feels like the most extraordinary thing I've ever done. It's impossible to overstate the joy and love that comes with having a child – every cliché feels true. In terms of philosophical questions, I've been thinking more about the fact that he will grow up in a world where he may never be more intelligent than AI. He'll never know what it's like to live without tools that aren't already incredibly smart and capable. The big thought I'm having is simply about how different the world is going to be for him, because of AI.

Imagine you will be there when our technology reaches AGI (Artificial General Intelligence) and you have the opportunity to be the first person to converse with it – what would you ask and why?

It would be to ask: how did we do it, how did we actually get to AGI? Or if we got to AGI very easily, I'd ask what the next challenges are that are in front of us and how do we get to what's next?

> "Having a baby feels like the most normal thing I've ever done, and in other ways, it feels like the most extraordinary thing I've ever done."

"If you can relax the constraints on intelligence and energy, I don't think we fully understand yet what that world will look like. However, I'm very excited to find out. It will be a world of great abundance."

But if you boiled it down to something specific, such as new technologies or energy, where would your mind go first?

Perhaps a new computing substrate – I'd assume that at the point we reach AGI, we'll also have abundant energy, so I'd love to know how to develop the next computer substrate.

At some point in a geopolitical conflict, your company and its technology may receive pressure from governments to work with them. How do you feel about this?

I expect there will be some pressure on us at some point. Still, I haven't given it a great deal of thought because the geopolitical landscape shifts significantly every year, and technology evolves rapidly as well. So, right now, the specific circumstances you're referring to are hard to predict.

How do you build a unique culture at OpenAI and truly convince every single team member that the sky is the limit?

==You can't do this with just one inspiring speech. You need to inspire people repeatedly, in every detail, in every meeting.== We're always asking people to go just that little bit further, think about a problem a little bit more expansively, and importantly, to try something that feels just that little bit riskier. When you do this enough, when you repeat it again and again, you eventually develop this emergent property.

Do you think that we are psychologically ready for the scale of change that AI could bring?

I have a tremendous belief in our ability to adapt to new things. Also, as humans, I think we can get badly psychologically hacked, and so we need to be vigilant against that.

Spencer Bailey

FOUNDER OF THE SLOWDOWN

Through The Slowdown and Time Sensitive, Bailey has emerged as a leading advocate for slower, more thoughtful media. Combining deep experience in design journalism with a uniquely personal lens on memory and culture, he's ideally placed to help shape a future where creativity is defined by depth rather than speed.

The key to the success of Colorado-born, New York-based writer, editor, and entrepreneur Spencer Bailey has been built on the idea that being first isn't always best. As co-founder of the media company The Slowdown and host of the globally respected Time Sensitive podcast, he champions intentionally 'slow', quality journalism in an era of content overload. A belief that taking time to reflect on important topics and conversations leads to more meaningful storytelling has helped Bailey build a catalogue of work that stands the test of time.

While Bailey, who grew up with expansive western vistas of the Rocky Mountains, has always been a big picture thinker, he notes that in New York in the 2010s – where he worked as editor-in-chief for design magazine *Surface* – he became dissatisfied with the relentless media cycle. He watched audiences gorge on what he likens to a 'fast-food' diet of digital content – cheaply produced, addictive, but non-nourishing journalism. Convinced of a better approach, The Slowdown became his forum for producing thought-provoking essays, interviews, curated guides, and podcasts, favouring depth over speed and delivering more meaningful narratives to a discerning audience.

Part of Bailey's reverence for time is rooted in personal history. In 1989, at age three, he survived a devastating plane crash – an accident that claimed 112 lives, including his mother's, and seared an awareness of life's fragility into his psyche. A famous photograph of his rescue that day was later cast in bronze as a public memorial in Sioux City, Iowa, effectively making Bailey part of a monument before he was old enough to understand its meaning. That early brush with tragedy instilled in him a profound appreciation for the weight of a moment and the importance of memory.

It's fitting that Bailey has become a thoughtful international voice on the long view: remembering and honouring the past, pondering the present, and looking toward the future. In his 2020 book, *In Memory Of: Designing Contemporary Memorials* (Phaidon), he explores the art and architecture of remembrance – from grand monuments to quietly powerful installations. As someone who writes extensively about design and architecture, he brings a unique sensitivity to how physical spaces can hold collective memory. His work on memorials underscores a central theme of his career: that how we mark the passage of time is fundamental to the human experience.

Seeing as your company's name is The Slowdown and your popular podcast is Time Sensitive, *I'm guessing time is important to you. When did you start thinking about slowing things down? Was that always your philosophy? Or was that philosophy born from a reaction to how you lived and worked, having had a career in fast-paced media?*

Growing up in Colorado, I had access to some of the most beautiful places in the world from birth. As a kid, growing up in nature, time slowed for me. I gained a deep relationship with time through the sun, because I grew up in the suburbs of Denver, looking towards the Rockies from our back window. Because of the landscape, because of where the mountains were, you always knew which way was west, so I learnt to tell the time by looking at the sun in relation to my environment – the sun became my clock. The sun became my way of following time and functioned as a compass. Even today in New York, I'll get out of the subway and automatically know which direction I need to go based on my general understanding of what time it is and where the sun is.

Fast-forward twenty years from my childhood, I was running *Surface* magazine and living this fast-paced media life in New York. At this point, I felt the time-blinkered nature of what it means to exist not just literally within a busy news cycle but also within New York City. From a geological and philosophical perspective, I started thinking about being more 'time-full' in my relationship to time, not just thinking about time from an industrial or nine-to-five perspective. This is where the idea for The Slowdown, which launched in 2019, came from.

I wasn't alone in this view; everyone working in media in the 2010s felt this rapid speed-up of information and this clickbait culture as digital media expanded. To me, there had to be a different way. I started thinking about the notion of 'slow media', similar to the 'slow food' movement. From the 1950s onwards, we saw this constant march of fast food, TV dinners, and frozen meals, ultimately leading to this loveless relationship with our food. The same became true of the media over time. In the 2010s, people consumed media almost thoughtlessly, resulting in them not feeling all that great about it. It was almost like bloat. ==You feel bloated consuming fast media, just like you feel bloated when you eat a bunch of Chicken McNuggets.==

I had this idea that The Slowdown could be an alternative mode of media-making that doesn't prescriptively consider time. I'm not telling people how to use their time, or if I am, it's subtly, through the lens of some of the leading creative voices of our time.

==**"Journalism, at its best, is a caregiving craft rooted in human connection and conversation."**==

Do you have a positive outlook about the future of media more broadly?

What will happen is a massive split between human-generated storytelling and machine-generated storytelling, so human-made journalism becomes almost like a Michelin-starred experience. While there's something sad about human-made journalism becoming a luxury product, it also means it will survive, as there will always be people willing to pay for it. Some generous billionaires might also want to fund free human-made journalism for the masses too.

Thinking about your question, the phrase that comes to mind is from Richard Fisher's book *The Long View*: 'nihilistic hope'. I love this term, which I hadn't heard until I read it in his book. But more people should know about it because it is precisely the phrase that captures our time concerning media. We're living in a moment of nihilistic hope – at least I am. It often feels like the sky is falling or, in the case of the media industry, that it's falling apart, but at the same time, I see a significant amount of hope and creative ideas bubbling up and being generated.

Journalism, at its best, is a caregiving craft rooted in human connection and conversation. You can create a podcast hosted by artificial intelligence, but it will never be the same as my podcast, where I sit down in the studio – in person, with a guest across from me – and have a real, true human exchange of ideas.

What other creative/technological opportunities does the future hold? What are you particularly excited about?

I have a lot of thoughts on this, and I have concerns too. From a research perspective, what's most exciting is AI's ability to pull information that would generally require hours of research to find – it will create all sorts of efficiencies. That said, there are certain things that AI can't do. I once listened to this compelling interview with Sam Altman, the CEO of OpenAI, who's at the forefront of this technology. He talked about how the value of craft – truly well-crafted objects and art – will increase exponentially as AI becomes more prevalent. That's something that AI can't do. This is a creative opportunity.

For my *Time Sensitive* podcast, I interviewed Malcolm Gladwell, the writer who popularised the '10,000-hour rule' in his book *Outliers*. His theory is that achieving expertise in any field requires roughly 10,000 hours of practice. I asked him, "What will happen in a world where AI will eliminate steps two through seven in these 10,000 hours? Will it take less time to become a master?" The answer to me is that ==AI probably won't help you become a master in less than 10,000 hours, but it will create shortcuts== in becoming what we deem, say, a 'good journalist' today. AI will dramatically impact so many business sectors we can't fathom. The question becomes, "How will the world's future leaders get to C-suite positions if AI eliminates many of the old steps one has traditionally had to learn to get there? Should AI replace human experience?"

Your work often focuses on responding to design and the built environment. You've authored books on architecture and profiled architectural greats over the years. How will AI affect the idea of a master architect or master of design?

It will affect it in the same way that it will affect journalism. In media, you will have free AI content on one side and human-made storytelling behind a paywall. In architecture, you might see something similar; you'll still have the masters, the Peter Zumthors of the world, doing very high-craft, expensive architecture that starts with a human sketch or a watercolour painting. On the other hand, you'll have very cheap, efficient ways of building, making architecture, and designing.

This dialogue can get dark fast. You start thinking about who's going to design the prisons of the future, who's going to design the military bunkers of the future? This is what AI is going to do. It's going to create the future McDonald's. It is going to transform our cityscapes in ways that are appalling and horrible. There will also always be places for urban planners and architects who lead with the hand and the heart. These two very polar things will soon be occurring at the same time and sometimes meeting in the middle. If there's anybody who's anti-AI, they're fooling themselves. We are going to live in a world that is prolific with AI. It's how we use it and when we use it that matters. It should be used to generate incredible creative growth instead of just replacing the human head, hand, and heart.

Thinking about the next generation. Do you feel that human impulse to create and be freely artistic will continue to linger? Will kids still live impoverished lives as architecture and fashion students in New York, to soak up its creative energy and be inspired, or do you think creativity will be drilled out of us more and more by the algorithm?

I don't think so, because there will always be a place for art at the end of the day, and how we define art will evolve and expand beyond how we've traditionally thought of it from the pedestal or the museum wall. Art will become more potent than AI's work in all of its applied ways. I'm more of an 'and both' believer in AI and humans colliding in exciting ways. The main thing is that AI should never ultimately usurp human creativity; there's still friction within the human brain when you're in the creative process. This friction creates beautiful things and results in some of our most significant works of art and architecture, from the pyramids to Norman Foster's Hearst Tower in New York.

Professionally speaking, how do you define your guiding principles?

Growing up, my dad had this bumper sticker on one of our cars, a tagline for Ben & Jerry's: "If it's not fun, why do it!?" To me, that's huge. When fun and joy start leaving the room, it's time to recalibrate and think about what you're doing and why. That's always been a guiding principle for me.

I also live with a certain ethic, or 'time' ethic; I try not to overwork. It's hard because I think people like me, who have a creative impulse that won't die, go a little overboard sometimes! I have to catch myself when this happens. Quite ironically, I have to tell myself to slow down. It's strange. I founded this company called The Slowdown a year before the pandemic. We found ourselves in a global slowdown, and yet The Slowdown did not slow down in the slowdown.

"We are going to live in a world that is prolific with AI. It's how we use it and when we use it that matters. It should be used to generate incredible creative growth instead of just replacing the human head, hand, and heart."

Finally, many of your anecdotes come from when you were much younger. Reflecting on time seems to be a big part of your creative process. I'd love to hear a bit more about that.

Yes, it's interesting. I was just reading another incredible book, *Immemorial* by Lauren Markham. It's a long-form essay contemplating how we think about memory and memorialisation in a climate crisis. That's important because embedded in that is all life and how we process what's been lost and what can be saved of what we still have.

It's hard to answer your question because I live in a constant state of reflection, but I try not to get too wound up in it. For me, it's not just deeply personal; it's also collective. I argue that, in our brief time on earth, we should embrace ambiguity and the unknown. Having a carpe diem mindset could sound cheesy, but I've always lived that way because a month before my fourth birthday I survived a plane crash that took my mother's life. She was among 112 people who died in the crash. I knew from that day that every day could be your last.

Surviving that crash, it was almost like being reborn into that perspective. We're not naturally born with such a perspective. Something occurs, and then a perspective is formed. In my case, it was surviving this traumatic, life-changing event and learning how to grow in the face of that adversity. In a certain sense, I've always thought of the planet as – this is a very Isamu Noguchi-Buckminster Fuller idea – a plane. Buckminster Fuller called it 'Spaceship Earth'. For me, the metaphor of a plane crash to understand our current climate situation is spot on.

"When fun and joy start leaving the room, it's time to recalibrate and think about what you're doing and why."

In the case of United Airlines Flight 232, which I was on, it was a small crack in a piece of metal in a fan disk that expanded over time and then eventually burst. And I was on the plane when it burst 37,000 feet in the air, over Nebraska cornfields. That understanding that something as small as a crack could expand over time and then just burst – that's the climate crisis. That is what we're facing. And this expands on your reflection question, I think that at the heart of what I'm trying to do is raise awareness around different ways of thinking about not just time, but our limited time on this planet, and how we can all not only make the most of it but leave a better planet for those to come – to be a good ancestor.

Jonathan Berte

Berte has transformed artificial intelligence from academic theory into practical technology, applying computer vision and machine learning to revolutionise fields from agriculture to advanced medicine.

CHAIRMAN AND FOUNDER OF ROBOVISION

As founder of Robovision, Jonathan Berte has spent the last decade and a half bringing artificial intelligence out of the lab and into the real world. Over fifteen years ago, his Belgium-based company began by automating manual labour in horticulture, putting computer vision and robotics to work in greenhouses. Since then, Robovision's AI platform has expanded into an array of industries – from helping to quality check cutting-edge semiconductors to detecting tiny tumours in oncology – all with a mission of augmenting human capabilities with intelligent machines. Berte's pioneering work exemplifies human-technology integration: using AI to transform traditional fields and solve practical problems at scale. He is also engaged with initiatives exploring the philosophical and societal consequences of emerging intelligence; a reflection of his belief that AI transformation must be met with equally deep inquiry into governance, ethics, and human purpose.

Berte has been immersed in neural networks and machine learning since the late 1990s, long before these technologies grabbed global headlines. This future-focused mindset is matched by an entrepreneurial philosophy geared towards disruption. Berte believes in challenging the status quo and iterating towards bold goals – he emphasises the importance of defining a clear 'North Star' vision even when the future is uncertain. In practice, his innovation playbook involves assembling lean but high-impact teams. This focused conviction helped Robovision stay ahead of the curve as AI went from academic curiosity to a global force.

Berte's foresight extends to the societal scale. He is convinced that AI's rise will disrupt every industry – and indeed every facet of society – in ways we are only beginning to grasp. He believes advanced AI could upend the traditional five-day workweek paradigm and even suggests we may need to reinvent the nation-state itself to keep up with technological change. For Berte, this isn't sci-fi speculation but a logical extrapolation of current trends: he sees today's breakthroughs as the start of a seismic shift that could 'transform humanity into another degree of civilisation'. In his view, such disruption demands equally bold innovation in how we govern, educate, and organise society at a systems level.

Yet even as he heralds AI's transformative potential, Berte maintains that humans must remain firmly in the loop. In his view, there are fundamental limits to what AI can achieve on its own – for instance, the next leaps in intelligence may require humans to reinvent the underlying hardware and make deliberate choices about the 'substrate' on which AI runs. He argues that AI can advise and automate, but people still need to steer the ship, whether that means building new infrastructure or managing the local impact of an AI-driven project. Berte also tempers his optimism with warnings about social cohesion and equity: if society can't adapt to the pace of technological change, power imbalances could widen and many people could be left behind. He stresses that preserving the social 'glue' in an AI-augmented world is as important as the innovation itself.

By combining radical vision with pragmatic thoughtfulness, Jonathan Berte personifies the ethos of future-shaping leadership. His insistence on anticipating the future, embracing disruption, and driving human-centric technological innovation at a societal scale makes him a natural fit for Ahead of Time's exploration of foresight and change.

Please give a brief overview of how you pitch Robovision – how you explain it to the public – and the role AI plays in the company as it develops.

I'm the founder of Robovision. Robovision started out as an image-processing robotics company. The first project we did in horticulture was more than fifteen years ago, so we disrupted that ecosystem of manual labour in difficult circumstances – greenhouses with lots of tedious work. From that success emerged the need for an AI platform where the end customer (a business, in our case) is fully enabled to create and maintain AI. Suppose you're an OEM, a machine builder, or a microscopy vendor. In that case, you contact Robovision to get an OEM component that, with a bit of integration, can automatically detect things, do quality control, or pick items. That's, in a nutshell, what we do at Robovision. The spectrum of our work goes from replacing hand labour to visual quality control. For example, some of the most advanced chips in the world are tested with Robovision, and in oncology, we detect the smallest tumours in the brain to help people survive cancer. We're active across this vast landscape of transforming visual information into an action or an insight.

How have you seen the technology improve and how far can it go?

It has improved night and day – extremely dramatically – with the revolution of convolutional neural networks (also called deep learning). This revolution is still not done, because we're still in the first iteration of convolutional neural networks. We now have transformers, and we're moving to new, more reinforcement-learning-based architectures. But it's all fresh in the broader context of humanity's technological history. It could elevate humanity to a new phase of civilisation; another league, so to speak, in which we may soon be playing. I've been there since the early days: in 1999 at the Institute of Neuroinformatics in Zurich, my colleagues were reverse-engineering the mammalian brain based on cat brains. That was very academic – it was far-fetched work that nobody outside of a few institutes cared about. But gradually, people started recognising the sheer power of these networks, and AlexNet in 2012 was pivotal. Things really took off with Yoshua Bengio's lab in Montreal, Geoffrey Hinton, and of course Yann LeCun. It's been a rocky decade from that perspective, and I'm glad I could play a small part in the history of AI.

"We're still in this mantra of the industrial revolution, where we go to work and then have some leisure time – five days of work, two days of rest. AI will ultimately disrupt that concept and lead us to a new work-life balance that makes more sense."

One area you've been ahead of the curve in is integrating AI into real work – into the kinds of skills humans have been doing for a long time. In terms of shaping the workforce (for example, I work in media and communications and it's amazing how quickly we've adopted these tools), do you think every single industry is going to be impacted in a massive way by AI, in ways we can't even imagine yet? Is it inevitable – because it boosts productivity and profit so much – that eventually no aspect of work will remain untouched by AI?

Absolutely. I'm a true believer in the power of AI to disrupt entire ecosystems. We've seen such disruptions firsthand. In horticulture, in the beginning everything was very labour-oriented, with almost medieval conditions for planting. We introduced neural networks there about ten years ago. It has been flabbergasting to see how eighteen-year-olds with only a secondary-school degree can create an AI model and then let a robot run on plants they've never seen before. AI is already disrupting sectors in ways we're only beginning to grasp and its long-term impact may be even more profound. We're still in this mantra of the industrial revolution, where we go to work and then have some leisure time – five days of work, two days of rest. AI will ultimately disrupt that concept and lead us to a new work-life balance that makes more sense. This shift will likely require rethinking aspects of the nation-state model, particularly how we deliver education, healthcare, and infrastructure in a world of decentralised, AI-driven productivity.

Those are two massive ideas you're putting forward. And you obviously like to work – you love working and building companies. For you personally, is the idea of a shift to a more relaxed, less work-centric lifestyle actually a positive?

It is, but it depends on the personality. Some people will embrace nature and spend much more time with friends and family. Others will go into the lab and invent a string of new products on their own in a matter of weeks. We live in a world where the possibilities are endless. We have access to more information than a president had even two decades ago. We have access to more academic courses than a billionaire's kid did ten years ago. ==Personal wisdom is going to be quintessential – and thus education and everything around it.== Right now our educational system is preparing kids and adolescents for roles which will not exist a couple of years from now. That is what I mean by disruption of the nation-state. We have these state entities that ensure you have healthcare, education, and infrastructure (they pave the roads with your taxes). But we all feel that this model is at a breaking point. Look at Trump yesterday – Silicon Valley just told him to back off, and even someone like Trump said, "Okay." In many countries, we already see hybrid governance dynamics, where large corporations exert outsized influence on democratic processes and technological policy. In the end, though, it's AI that will be the ultimate enabler of so much wealth that it will disrupt things for everybody on this planet.

Do you see places where things are a little more controlled – like Singapore or the Emirates – actually having the upper hand here? If nations are going to change entirely, is it the smaller, more nimble countries that will get ahead of the big, bulky bureaucratic places like the UK? These shifts aren't going to happen overnight, are they?

What we've seen is that geopolitical shifts cannot happen overnight – unless you have a war – but technological shifts can happen overnight. We all saw the 'DeepSeek' moment when it launched and immediately triggered a $1 trillion sell-off in the global market, simply because it implied you'd need fewer semiconductors to create stellar AI. So there's a difference between technological disruption and geopolitical disruption. To your point about smaller countries being more agile, more like speedboats compared to nation-states like the UK: it's certainly true. But we shouldn't underestimate the role of institutions, this mesh we call democracy, in shaping or slowing those changes. As someone who has founded a technology enterprise from the ground up, I appreciate the necessity of that process, even when it feels slow. I just think that the frequency, the pace, the neck-breaking speed at which everything is evolving is no longer compatible with the typical duration of government. Even the United Nations doesn't have much say over everything that's happening in the world. We need to come up with another fabric of our global society, and let's hope we don't have to go through a war before we gain new wisdom and insights. Things do look a bit edgy nowadays.

"Humans will always remain extremely important … We cannot go beyond a certain stage of AI, in either training or inference, if we don't fundamentally disrupt the hardware on which it's trained."

Jonathan Berte

With all this in mind, as a business leader – and touching on the questions we're asking everyone in this series – how do you define your guiding principles?

My first principle is never accept the status quo. Innovation starts from challenging what everyone assumes to be true, and that's how Robovision was founded. Our aim was to disrupt a very stable and conservative ecosystem of industrial automation. Everybody swore by optical sensors and PLCs (Programmable Logic Controllers), and we disrupted that by replacing them with a PC and cameras – which was unheard of fifteen years ago in a robotics context. The second is to surround yourself with passionate 10x profiles and keep your team small and agile. ==You don't need big teams to disrupt society; I strongly believe that with the tools we have nowadays this is more true than ever.== The third is always to pursue a clear North Star. Whatever you do should align with a mission you deeply care about. That will align with two other things: it creates a framework for disruption (principle one) and it attracts very smart people, because they see a clear mission. Those are basically the rules that I follow.

How do you create a North Star when you're not even sure what the future is going to be? How did you do that with Robovision?

Very early on, we felt that neural networks were going to disrupt a hell of a lot of things, because we saw how we ourselves were being disrupted. The North Star is this: you look at the asymptote of how something is going to evolve, and you know that in the beginning it's difficult to engineer – you need a team of extremely talented people to navigate those initial complexities. But we know this trajectory is headed toward simplification and commoditisation. So your North Star has to do with how you'll position yourself in that commoditised landscape. You have to reason: do we focus on a set of verticals where we create value for specific ecosystems (healthcare, silicon, agriculture), or do we stay as an engine that is neutral to the topic of disruption at stake?

Quite a big-lens approach, then. It's always a moving target. And you need to have something like a target – otherwise how do you perceive it moving?

We're asking everyone about the next big thing in their field. Anyone not working in AI would probably say AI is the next big thing. But for you, in AI – your understanding of it is far more profound than the everyday person's – what would you say is the next big thing that most people aren't thinking about yet? We're now in a world of ChatGPT and large language models, but I'm sure you're thinking well beyond that. Are we already seeing advances in areas like military hardware and is that where it's going to start? Are you implying there's a future for human engineers themselves, or will we just sit back and let robots build our future when it comes to hardware?

No. Humans will always remain extremely important for the next layer of disruption, because they need to decide to change the substrate – to change the ecosystem. We cannot go beyond a certain stage of AI, in either training or inference, if we don't fundamentally disrupt the hardware on which it's trained. That is ultimately a human decision, because it involves, say, building a factory on a piece of land. AI will advise us to do so, and it might even generate the plans. But ultimately, we need to manage the local community and convince them that it will be good for them, then manage the environment. Even there, we'll have AI advising us – for example, "You'll need these toxic chemicals here, so you should plan to mitigate the risks." ==In the end, AI has the potential to become the ultimate enabler of prosperity, unlocking unprecedented wealth==, but it will profoundly affect the way we live, work, and govern ourselves.

Earlier you mentioned a renewed emphasis on leisure in some people's lives, because technology is taking away a lot of life's arduous tasks. Are you genuinely optimistic about the future? When you turn on the news and see all the rubbish with politics and constant negativity – and then climate change on top of that – how do you feel about the future? You're always thinking ahead, so I wonder if you're optimistic or not.

From a possibilities perspective, I'm profoundly optimistic. We have more opportunities at our fingertips than at any point in human history. But we must be careful since opportunity and upheaval often come hand in hand. At the same time, I'm a bit wary of the fabric of society as a whole. We've gone through very big crises before, and the last huge crisis – World War II – was followed by flourishing decades because so much manual labour was needed to rebuild and create consumer goods. The labourers in the factories could ultimately afford to buy those goods themselves (think of the German *Wirtschaftswunder*). If we were to face such a crisis again, I don't know if that glue is still there, because in a philosophical way labour has been the glue between the rich and the poor. The rich need the poor as consumers and as builders in their factories, and the poor need the rich as investors. There was almost this Marxist equilibrium in society that kept everything cohesive. What we see in nation-states right now is that technology is generating a delta where people in power can use technology to become much smarter than the other half of society. That is far more risky than it was 50 or 100 years ago – especially with military technology. We're at the beginning of an awakening in Europe where we realise we need our own missile industry and advanced arms. Of course, Europe has a lot of smart people who will create even more sophisticated weapons than those made by a Northrop Grumman or a Lockheed Martin. But what will it mean if those arms are bought by a nation-state that doesn't have kind intentions towards its people?

Going back to the idea of technology taking things away from people – you're talking about the post-war rebuild and industry. I was listening to a podcast yesterday about this lost generation of mainly young men for whom, essentially, there is no factory job anymore. There's nothing for them. It's already quite a bleak picture, seeing what's happening to these young men who are being left behind in society, and we're only at the beginning of it. Does this mean we have our work cut out for us to support people who risk being left behind by rapid technological progress? How do we fix this?

Indeed. I *want* to be positive, and I think my optimism is mostly explained by the possibilities. We can go anywhere with humanity right now, but if we take the wrong turn, that could be a dire rabbit hole.

How are you enabling positive possibilities in your work environment – in the team culture you're building and in the way you act as a leader?

I believe in keeping our organisation flat, collaborative, and driven by curiosity. I enjoy thinking far into the future alongside my team, and I resist adding needless layers of hierarchy. At the end of the day, we're not just cogs in a corporate machine, we're innovators shaping tomorrow and we should enjoy the journey together.

> "From a possibilities perspective, I'm profoundly optimistic …
> But at the same time, I'm a bit wary of the fabric of society as a whole."

Jonathan Berte

Luca de Meo

De Meo's three decades of leadership experience at automotive giants, including Renault, have shaped his expertise in operational transformation and emotional brand-building. He's now using this know-how to shape the future of luxury at Kering.

CHIEF EXECUTIVE OFFICER AT KERING

For over thirty years, Luca de Meo carved a path of success across some of the world's most renowned automotive brands – from Toyota and Fiat to the Volkswagen Group and, most recently, with the top job at Renault. In the process, he gained a masterful understanding of the mobility industry, as well as product design and brand strategy. In mid-2025, his career took a new turn as he transitioned into the world of high fashion and luxury, becoming the Chief Executive Officer of Kering, one of Europe's leading luxury conglomerates. It was a move from cars to the catwalk, but one grounded in the same principles of innovation and brand excellence that have defined his career. When this conversation took place, de Meo was at a professional crossroads: he was preparing to step away from Renault – the century-old French automaker he had revitalised with a bold, brand-led approach – and embrace a new challenge outside the car industry, making it the best time to discuss the future of business.

After all, this is a man with a knack for drawing upon informed foresight to steer corporate agendas. In the past, he has been able to chart a course ahead by pre-empting changing consumer habits, as evidenced by his transformative work in the automotive industry. He had arrived at Renault in 2020 when the company was veering towards a multibillion-euro annual loss, and within a few years, he steered it back to success. De Meo's revitalisation plan reorganised the business around its authentic brand identity, moving Renault's line-up decidedly upmarket in the process. Leading Kering is, in many ways, a natural next step for de Meo. Kering – the European luxury group behind Gucci and Saint Laurent – is another powerhouse built on heritage brands and global consumer appeal. Guiding an organisation steeped in creative legacy plays to de Meo's brand-centric leadership style and cultural intuition.

This future-focused discussion spans topics from building strong teams and adaptive organisations to the value of heritage in a fast-changing world. Key insights from the conversation include de Meo's perspective on designing flexible organisational models that can adapt quickly to market changes, the importance of human-centred leadership even amid rapid technological advancements, and his informed views on how the mobility landscape will look in the years to come.

How would you describe your approach to leadership and team building?

The ingredients are always the same. You need to have a certain sense of the people around you. People like us should be good at understanding each person's talent and genius and putting it at the service of a project. You could use the metaphor of a chef who opens the fridge and sees what's inside, and then tries to imagine what dish they can create with it. Most of the time, you don't have everything you need, so you have to be good at combining different ingredients and different spices. This is 30% of our job – selecting people, identifying their qualities and their weaknesses (everybody has some), and then trying to combine them properly.

You also have to be able to take a bird's-eye view of your organisation. Like a falcon, you fly high above the action, and from time to time, you see a rabbit, and then you dive down. But you can't stay down all the time. You can't micromanage all the time. You must micromanage when you identify an issue. And then after fixing it, you move back to hundred, two hundred metres so that you can see the big picture. You have people who are comfortable on the ground, or people who are relaxed up high, but not many people are comfortable at both. And what I have always seen in great leaders throughout my career is their ability to do both micro and macro-level work simultaneously.

How do you design an organisation that can adapt to change?

After selecting the right people, the second part is designing an organisation – and by extension, its processes – where people can express all their energy. Sometimes, very good people get killed by the organisation or by established methods. ==You must always consider not only the people, but also the structure and the model.== Think of it like football: people in my position have two key opportunities. One is to decide which team starts the game. The second step is to determine the type of strategy you want to apply. In the past, companies would often adhere to a single model; however, the world is moving so quickly that you now need the ability, like in professional sports, to adapt the model even within the game. This is also true for organisations. I tend to design an organisation with a pencil rather than casting it in marble.

==“History provides a wealth of inspiration for creativity. Europe remains one of the regions where significant innovation continues to emerge across various industries.”==

Professionally speaking, how do you define your guiding principles?

Beyond my job, I'm passionate about cars. I'm a car freak. So, my attention has always been on this product – I'm a product person, and everywhere I have been in my career, this passion for products has followed me. Of course, I understand that other things are essential for the company, but at the end of the day, it's a product that customers are paying us for.

Secondly, ==I have fought my entire career to keep the 'e' of emotion in the business equation.== I have long rallied against the commoditisation of the automobile. Sure, some customers might not know the difference between a Peugeot and a Renault, but many more buy a car because of the emotion it brings – and the brand creates that emotion. I have been fighting my whole life to create emotional products.

I also push an organisation to focus on what is essential for the consumer. At Renault Group, we decided that brands, not functions or regions, should drive the company. Brands in our business – like Alpine and Mobilize – naturally push us to a specific target consumer community. And for the people in our company managing these brands, we pay them on margins, not volumes, and customer satisfaction. In this way, we have the customer in focus all the time.

> "I tend to design an organisation with a pencil rather than casting it in marble."

How will artificial intelligence change the way we work?

I'm pretty relaxed about it. There was a lot of debate – will AI replace humans, when will we reach the singularity, etc.? It's overstated. In the tech industry, they often create a wave and pump it up so much that you feel like this thing is crucial and everyone has to jump on it. Sometimes we've seen these things fizzle out.

I feel it's the same kind of thing with AI. People say it will completely transform our lives. However, consider that we had mobile phones and the internet changing our lives in the 2000s, and now we have AI entering the picture. People still get married, have children, and play sports – at the end of the day, life goes on. These tools tend to speed up human activities and make them easier. Apart from some exceptions, they mainly improve the quality of people's lives. I always see technology as a tool rather than an end in itself. We utilise AI, and we will continue to do so. I'm convinced it will improve productivity. It's like putting a turbocharger on an engine: from the same displacement, you get a lot more power.

AI is going to permeate organisations and automate many things, not only physical tasks but also intellectual tasks. It is to white-collar work what robots have been to manufacturing. That means it will replace people in some activities, but then those individuals will find more suitable jobs or new opportunities. Refusing technological progress has never been a smart strategy for any society. Of course, we must implement it responsibly and consider the ethical implications, but we're not going to eliminate knives because some people misuse them in crime – we all need knives to cut our food. I believe AI will have a significant impact on the way we work. It will free us up to do things we didn't have time for when we were busy with tasks that AI can now cover. I don't call it artificial intelligence, because that term can be misleading – I call it augmented intelligence. It's a tool.

How do you balance a brand's heritage with innovation?

Every time I came into an automotive company, the first thing I did was try to internalise the values of the organisation and understand its history. These companies have a very strong culture, and if you come in and say, "At my old company we did it like this", it never works – the system will resist, because those values and practices have been built over decades by thousands of people. ==What I try to do is always first get the values and the history under my skin, and only then give a personal touch to it.== That's how I do it. And I've always tended to take brands and make them upmarket. Secondly, I always try to keep the emotion in the equation. You wouldn't see me working in a B2B environment – those are less emotional products. I enjoy working in consumer industries because I have the opportunity to connect with people's emotions.

That's where I'm good. If you put me in front of the consumer, in front of the market, I understand – I'm a good marketer. Good marketers can put themselves in the shoes of other people and try to give them something that either they expect, or, if you're very good, something they don't know they want. But when you show it to them, they start dreaming about it. The minimum you can do is fulfil people's expectations; the best thing you can do is surprise them in a positive way, because they never thought about what you're selling, but they love it. It's about curiosity, intellectual humility, and learning.

==**"I don't call it artificial intelligence, because that term can be misleading – I call it augmented intelligence. It's a tool."**==

At Renault, how did you discuss designing for the future without forgoing the all-important brand codes and DNA that have contributed to the company's success over the past 125 years?

This is something deeply rooted in the way the company operates. A Renault designer – someone who has been there for ten years – will instinctively know where to place the design elements, the buttons, the details. Of course, there are holy books on how you design a Renault, just like there are holy books for BMW. But beyond that, it's an intuitive understanding – people just know what Renault is and what it isn't. And in the case of a company with a long tradition, you have this deep design cave – a reservoir of stories and references that nurture the brand's legend. Think about the Renault 5, the Renault 4, the Alpine models. That's something new brands simply cannot do. If you look at what's happening in China, many companies hire designers from established brands, but it takes generations to build a real design identity. Sometimes, you don't even recognise a Chinese car by its shape – you must check the logo to know what it is.

==One of the advantages we have in Europe is a deep, holistic understanding of branding – including the product's aesthetics.== You can immediately recognise a Bic pen without thinking about it. You can't easily teach or code that into a design process. Of course, there are rules to follow, but at the end of the day, it's about culture, and it's about time.

Of course, engineers – who might want to tweak the design to improve aerodynamics – and designers trying to protect the brand identity always discuss it. If something doesn't look like a Renault, or even more drastically, if something doesn't look like a Ferrari, then the process naturally stops. Why? Because the culture embedded in the organisation acts as a safeguard. It ensures that the brand's identity isn't compromised.

Is this a positive aspect for all European brands when forecasting the future?

Absolutely, absolutely. Consistency is definitely one of our advantages – for the time being, especially when it comes to selling cars here in the Western world. People here understand brands differently.

If you go to China, you will see that they do a lot of incredible work – really great stuff – but sometimes, it can seem confusing. Every time manufacturers there come up with a new product, they often invent an entirely new brand to accompany it. And for them, that feels natural. It's a new product, so it deserves a new identity.

But we in Europe think differently, right? A brand is more than just a name – it's a system of thought, an experience, a framework that encodes a whole world of values. Even when we do new things, we tend, as Europeans, to maintain consistency in what we do.

Take Benoît Mintiens and Ressence, for example. Of course, he's competing with brands like Audemars Piguet, Cartier, or Rolex, but he's created something new while maintaining a distinctly European approach. You can recognise a Ressence watch immediately. It occupies a unique space in the market – a mechanical watch whose mechanism is suspended in oil, giving it an almost digital aesthetic while remaining entirely analogue. Benoît is creating a new brand with a very European and very consistent approach.

> "Even when we do new things, we tend, as Europeans, to maintain consistency in what we do."

So newness and boldness can be a defining element of European brands moving forwards?

Sometimes people think that the strength of European brands stems from their hundred-year, hundred-and-fifty-year, or three-hundred-year history. But it's not as simplistic as that.

History provides a wealth of inspiration for creativity. Europe remains one of the regions where significant innovation continues to emerge across various industries. Then, the fact that we are unable to industrialise this and scale it is another story. However, you still have many things invented in Europe today. We don't have a problem with ideas. We instead have an issue of scale and industrialisation of those ideas.

When examining the number of patents, we can measure it in two dimensions: quantity and quality. You will see that Europe will have less quantity but higher quality. And we should first of all be aware of that, be proud of that. And of course, nurture that creativity, because it's there, and it comes from the fact that we are a region of the world where people speak twenty different languages, where history is 3,000 years old, where cuisine is different from one country to the other and even from one village to the other. That's the beauty of Europe.

"Regulations can push in one direction, but ultimately, I respect the customer's and the market's power to decide what works."

Moving back to automotive, what's 'the next big thing' in this industry and how might it impact our lives? How does it make you feel?

In cities, ideally, electric vehicles will become the majority, or even the only option allowed, due to environmental concerns. But that requires solving infrastructure challenges. That said, it's more feasible in densely populated areas, where infrastructure is used more intensively and can become profitable. The real question is: where will the charging infrastructure be built? In buildings, on the streets, or in centralised hubs around the city? We'll see. However, in urban areas, public charging infrastructure has a better chance of being viable and profitable.

I also believe some vehicles in certain environments will be operated autonomously. Take buses, for example. Most of the time, they run with very few passengers, and in many cases, ticket prices are heavily subsidised. That makes them both economically and ecologically inefficient. So, we can imagine public transportation shifting to smaller, automated vehicles. One of the key challenges in this sector is a shortage of drivers, so there's already a business case for automation. In the future, we could see autonomous minibuses with dynamic routing – capabilities that adapt their routes in real time based on demand, understanding where people are, and where they need to drive. Technically, this is already feasible. From a regulatory perspective, it would require standardisation, and we see China leading in this area. At the end of the day, what we need will be driven by people. You can't force people to do what they don't want to do. However, solutions that make sense and fit naturally into daily life have real potential.

The shift to electric technology will naturally force the system, meaning people's habits will change because electric cars are not designed for long-range driving. So the first question is: will we really have 100% electric cars, or will it be a mix of different technologies? Regulations can push in one direction, but ultimately, I respect the customer's and the market's power to decide what works.

If you look at China, they're probably one generation ahead in this transition, yet even they are reconsidering a purely electric future. Despite their competitive advantage – owning the supply chain, manufacturing footprint, etc. – they don't see electric cars as the only solution. They're reinvesting in plug-in hybrids, range extenders, and other alternatives because they make sense.

Marcus Engman

CHIEF CREATIVE OFFICER AT IKEA RETAIL

Engman reshaped IKEA's design culture, driving landmark collaborations and opening the brand's creative processes to the public. Now working both inside IKEA and independently through his creative agency, he continues to champion design as a tool for community-building and systemic change – pushing forwards the next evolution of democratic, accessible design.

Marcus Engman jokes that he comes from 'an unlucky background'. He was born into what he calls 'an IKEA family', in which both his parents worked at one time or another for the Swedish mega-brand. "The only thing I didn't want to happen was for me to start working for that company, because of course I wanted to rebel", he says today, with a broad smile on his face. As fate would have it, IKEA is the company where Engman has spent the vast majority of his career, and he now serves as the CCO of IKEA Retail.

Engman didn't go straight in at the top, however. He decided not to go to university, describing himself as a 'total autodidact', and instead took a job pushing trolleys at one of IKEA's vast out-of-town superstores in Sweden. He then worked in the communications and interior design departments at various outlets and even had a brief spell as a store manager before he was drafted in to work on design and product development. He was in this department in 1995, when IKEA first launched its Democratic Design mantra at the Milan furniture fair Salone del Mobile, a philosophy which has guided Engman throughout his career.

Then, in 2012, having spent a decade outside of the IKEA family building up his own successful retail design agency, Engman returned to the company to take on the role of Head of Design, the role his father was at that time vacating. Engman served in this position for six years and oversaw IKEA's transformation from a company known predominantly for its flat-pack furniture to a global brand with design at its core. Today he spends half his time on his Sweden and London-based design agency, SKEWED, and half of his time working for IKEA Retail as its CCO, which sees him look at the company's 'development plan for the future and the future of retail'.

There are few people in the world better qualified to speak about the future of retail and design. After all, in many ways, Engman has shaped the direction of travel in these sectors for the past decade and a half, through pioneering the product collaboration agenda as head of design at IKEA, as well as the research agenda around life at home at IKEA Retail, and Atelier100, its incubator for emerging designers. But, as we discovered during our conversation, Engman is not one to demand plaudits. "I'm not really about chasing those credit things," he says, "it should happen naturally."

Here, we discuss with Engman the importance of curiosity, the power of creative communities, and the role that designers can play in tackling climate change.

Professionally speaking, how do you define your guiding principles? What are the values that have led you throughout your career?

These are maybe more my personality rather than guiding principles, but they've become my principles over time. I try to stay humble. I try not to just jump straight into things, thinking that I know it all, because it's easy to do that when you have a bit of experience. But having that humility to say, "I don't actually know this at all" – that's my starting point. I try to ask how we might bring people in who are better and smarter. And then, I preach a lot about the importance of curiosity, not just for people, but for brands and companies as well. That force of nature to want to know, being curious about what's around the corner, what could be, and so forth. I'm a really curious person. If I'm not learning, I start to die in some way. So, humbleness and curiosity, I would say those have been my principles and that's how I try to work.

Alongside this, you have to have a people-first perspective and be interested in people. Most of the things I've done, I haven't designed them myself; I've made people come to new conclusions and helped them to be better than they think they are. That's creative leadership, which is always underestimated. A lot of people talk about leadership, but creative leadership is a different beast. You can't shy away from friction – you need to find that positive friction, between people and between topics, because at the end of the day that's the only way to create energy. If you want to have great ideas, you need energy, and energy is produced by friction.

IKEA introduced Democratic Design as a kind of tagline in 1995. What does that mean to you today? And how has that idea informed your approach to design throughout your career?

For me, it's been super important. It's something I truly believe in, not just at IKEA, but it comes down to my belief in design, and what we can and should do with it. When we brought the idea of Democratic Design into the world in 1995, there were three different aspects. So it was form, and then form follows function, as it does in Scandinavian design. But then we added the low price, asking: could we have accessibility to good ideas? It was really a revolution at the time.

Over the years, we added quality and sustainability to that original formula. So there are now these five dimensions of Democratic Design. It's a bit impossible to make a product with all five – and that's exactly what you want. As a designer or product developer, you want that impossible challenge. It's part of making the friction. There are so many things you see in design that are just making things incrementally better, instead of trying to make change for real. Democratic Design isn't about making things, it's about making things better in the world.

Does the term Democratic Design also hold within it a bit of a criticism of the rest of the design world? Was it also partly about pointing out that the wider design industry wasn't very democratic in its approach?

That wasn't intended. I try to never be against things; I want to be for things. I'm for democracy and I'm for the thought that good ideas should be for the many. For me, if each and every one of us has a limited time on earth, then you want to make the most out of it. So why would you make things that are just for the few, instead of making things that create a big change for the many? That's how simple it is for me.

There is also another side to Democratic Design that we usually don't talk about so much, which is about bringing everyone in on the topic. There are still some parts of the design industry that believe in the single genius solving problems. I've never seen that. In reality, maybe there's one person taking credit for things but there's never one person making them. So, how could we make it so that everybody feels like they're part of the process and an integral part of what we do? That's something we've been getting better at year by year at IKEA. That's part of the success of IKEA – people don't feel they're a part of a big machine, but feel they're important. It's hard in a big company, but one of my biggest tasks is to make that happen.

"I think we will see a big trend of togetherness, where people come together to solve things and to design as well."

Let's stay with that idea of opening up the design process, because you were instrumental in the creation of Atelier100 alongside H&M, which was a kind of design incubator in London. Why did you decide to launch that?

That was one of my pet projects, and one of the things I'm most proud of. It came from a place of frustration, and something we discovered we had in common with H&M. Working with and trying to source creative talent to a company like IKEA, I want to reflect the people we serve – there are many individuals and they are quite diverse. What I could see in the setup of the creative teams was that they were not at all diverse, and meeting up with the new students from design universities and other creative universities, I saw the same thing. We really wanted to change that. So, how could we make it easier for good creatives who don't have a family background to help them, and become a platform for that?

I was in Milan the other week and some of the designers who went through Atelier100 were there. Some are now world-famous. We had a great conversation. What they appreciated the most was the fact that they found a new community of people who they didn't know before and they learned so much from each other, maybe more than they learned from the companies that were involved in it. It was a great thing and I think it will most likely be reborn in a different way in the future.

> "If I'm not learning, I start to die in some way."

You were also instrumental in introducing creative collaborations with designers around the world, weren't you? Can you talk us through that and why you decided to push that?

For me, it's about that humble and curious approach again. I and others at IKEA felt that we had got a little stuck in how we define the home and what we could do for it. Does the world really need yet another chair or yet another sofa? It's always good to be inspired by completely different things. If we look at activities and interests in the home, instead of just how you furnish it, then you find a lot of shit happening inside the home. So, we found out, for instance, that most music is consumed in the home. How could we design in a better way for that? That turned into a lot of different collaborations, including one with Sonos, where we tried to democratise the pricing of speakers for the home. And there was also a collection with Teenage Engineering, which was about how you could connect your home and throw parties. All of those collections were about making change. Other brands do brand collaborations – I wasn't at all interested in making brands rub off on themselves. It just happens that some of these people that have big brands are really good – there's a reason they're big. And if you want to change things, you want to be with the people who are really good. It all started with just making great designs together and changing things.

I'd love to look now at the future. What for you is 'the next big thing' in your field or industry? You can take that to mean either retail or design.

First of all, I'm honestly not that interested in the next big thing. I've never been on the search for the next big thing. But one thing I see growing within the industry, in creativity in general in fact, is kind of the antidote to what is happening around the world right now, which is all about alienating people from each other. I think we will see a big trend of togetherness, where people come together to solve things and to design as well. I have a big sense of trust and belief in the new generation of creatives. They are working far more in communities than they are working as individuals, and they're looking for help from each other and building strength by building the communities they are in. That's truly a good thing and we should applaud, embrace, and try to support that in every possible way.

In terms of retail specifically as a sector, what are some of the more exciting developments you're expecting to see there? Will technology, like AI perhaps, play a role?

I'm always encouraged. There are an extreme number of problems out there to be solved, but there are also even more opportunities for solving them. What's important to me is that idea of Democratic Design – I believe that good ideas should belong to the many. The other thing I've really learnt lately is the efficiency of designing with people instead of for people. I still think in the design industry we're often trying to understand things and then design for those things, instead of just bringing people in and designing *with* them instead, which makes it even better and also more fun. It's challenging in a new way.

You mentioned that there are an extreme number of problems out there. I'm guessing that climate change is right at the top of your list. When it comes to that challenge, what are the opportunities you see for solving that?

Honestly, I put a lot of my time into that, especially lately. The biggest opportunity is the fact that a more sustainable life is a more affordable life. If you're doing things in a sustainable way, it will also be more affordable. If we could just get that to come through to people, far more would have a more sustainable lifestyle. But still, we live in a world where people think that sustainability comes at a premium. It does not and it should not. Then secondly, it's all of those small steps that you can make inside a company and become better. We have over 200,000 employees at IKEA. That's a small town, more or less. Then, if you add on top of that all of our suppliers, it's quite a big town suddenly, and if you can change their behaviour, it has a big impact. But that's nothing compared to what we can change if we can design and deliver in ways that nudge our roughly three billion visitors a year. That's changing the world. It's a big responsibility. That's what we try to design for – to nudge ourselves and other people's behaviour into something that is more sustainable.

"The biggest opportunity is the fact that a more sustainable life is a more affordable life. If you're doing things in a sustainable way, it will also be more affordable."

In your role as CCO of IKEA Retail, you spend a lot of time imagining the future of the brand and the future of retail in general. You may not be able to say too much about this, but what can we expect over the next few years from IKEA on the retail front?

You're going to see a lot of new formats and ways of meeting IKEA, because we have slowly but steadily understood that it's as important for us to come to where people are as it is to get people to come to where we are. The old IKEA concept was built on getting people to come to our blue boxes slightly outside of cities. That's still super strong, but we need to be better at coming to where they are, and also in different ways. That could be anything from pop-ups to city stores to new formats. So you're going to see us being more agile.

"You can't shy away from friction – you need to find that positive friction, between people and between topics, because at the end of the day that's the only way to create energy. If you want to have great ideas, you need energy, and energy is produced by friction."

Lastly, generally speaking, what creative opportunities does the future hold? What are you particularly excited about?

I'm going to be super personal on this one. I split my time between IKEA and my own design studio, SKEWED. We're launching a new brand ourselves now, which we will call Everything – everything for everyone at once. It's going to be really fun to see how people see it and what they're going to do with it. It's very much an optimistic and curious view around how you could make do with as few things as possible. That's what we're going to explore in wave after wave of product design. In big companies – and I work with IKEA, but also Decathlon, H&M, Volvo, and other super big companies – no matter how fast you are and how good you are, it's still a slow process. So the fun thing about having your own design agency and your own brand on the other side is that you can test a thing in a matter of months and see how people react, then make it bigger and better.

Tony
Fadell

Tony Fadell

Fadell created the iPod and co-founded smart home brand Nest, using intuitive, user-friendly design to simplify technology. Now, as an investor, he funds companies innovating in sustainable energy, food systems, and new materials – backing practical, design-driven solutions that directly address real human needs and some of society's most urgent global problems.

FOUNDER OF
BUILD COLLECTIVE

Tony Fadell's work is focused on creating a better future for us all. Nicknamed 'the father of the iPod', his time at Apple saw him create the device that changed how we think about personal audio – for the better. Engineer, entrepreneur, executive, investor, and inventor, Fadell is a polymath whose work is empowered by a contagious sense of optimism for humanity to do better and think bigger. This philosophy is felt across the companies he invests in and advises, currently through Build Collective, which supports innovative start-ups, guiding them from ambitious ideas to real-world solutions.

So what sort of world does this visionary see in fifteen years' time? Sitting down with Ahead of Time, Fadell lays out a roadmap for building a world where we travel more sustainably, live more meaningful lives in cleaner cities, and humans (not robots) continue to work hard to improve our lives. Fadell believes that achieving this isn't so much about pie-in-the-sky, never-dreamed-of-before ideas created as a novelty but about enhancing what already exists. Similarly to the iPod being a smart evolution from the portable CD and tape players from years past – we'll still fly in planes for future journeys. We'll just make these trips in a radically redesigned, much better aircraft.

Central to Fadell's approach is the idea that genuine innovation must target real-world problems; the 'pain points' people experience daily but have grown accustomed to ignoring. He sees enormous potential in transforming urban mobility through electrification, dramatically reducing fuel usage in travel, and integrating augmented reality more seamlessly into our everyday lives.

In what is presently a vital time for technological change – as AI plays an increasingly significant role in our lives – Fadell paints a picture of an age of innovation, marrying progress in this relatively new field with responsible stewardship, ensuring that today's innovations leave a positive imprint on future generations. As the conversation unfolds, readers will find reassuring optimism threaded throughout – an affirmation that the thoughtfully designed future is something to look forward to.

What creative/technological opportunities does the future hold? What are you particularly excited about?

AR glasses. We started with the Ray-Ban product, which was launched in 2023. I worked on Google Glass, so I had to reboot it, and everyone laughed at it. But what I was trying back then is precisely what Meta launched years later. The Apple Vision Pro will not be everywhere, but many will use AR glasses.

You've also said you see value in an invisibility cloak.

Yes, well, no one's come up with it yet, but we're going to want to be more and more private in the future. I have a mantra, 'you pay more to get less'; you go to a high-end hotel to get less of the world. You go to these ecotourism resorts that cost a lot more, so you get less of the developed world wanting to take all your attention. I believe people are going to want to try to have that around them at all times. And what's a device that can help you avoid everybody trying to get at you? What is it going to look like?

Looking ahead fifteen years, with a positive outlook, how do you envision life in your home city, Paris, and how will people live differently?

Paris had already undergone a fantastic transformation since I started coming here in 2009. Now, 15-16 years later, the changes are remarkable. There's more traffic, pollution, and noise in Miami than in what I call 'New Paris', even though Paris is a higher-density city. And this shift is only going to continue. Cities will become more liveable as we see a rise in battery-operated two- and three-wheeled light vehicles in dense urban areas.

You're already seeing it in places like New York, where congestion pricing is finally starting – something London has had for years. The United States has its challenges, but globally, cities are moving towards a more liveable future.

Will they become more social? That's uncertain. With digital displays everywhere and people already carrying them in their hands (smartphones), how we interact may continue to change. But one thing is clear: cities will be far more human than they were over the last 30, 40, or 50 years – an era dominated by streets filled with cars and trucks rather than people.

> "No one's come up with it yet, but we're going to want to be more and more private in the future. I have a mantra, 'you pay more to get less'; you go to a high-end hotel to get less of the world ... I believe people are going to want to try to have that around them at all times."

And will people be healthier?

Overall, health is evolving. In the United States, for example, there's a growing awareness that drinking is carcinogenic – similar to the shift we saw with smoking. We're also redefining obesity, and now you have drugs like Wegovy and Ozempic reshaping the conversation. There are even healthy foods marketed as 'Wegovy- and Ozempic-friendly'.

A hundred years ago, people were generally healthier in their daily lives than they are today, outside of illness and genetic predispositions. But now, we're heading towards a bifurcated society. In the past, most people followed a similar physical activity and diet baseline. Moving forwards, there will be a clear divide between those who actively maintain their health and those who don't.

The difference is that we now have the technology, information, and food systems to make healthier choices more accessible. Whether through smart glasses, wearable devices like rings, enhanced food labelling, or even delivery services, people will have more tools than ever to support a healthier lifestyle. That doesn't necessarily mean healthy choices will be cheaper, but making better decisions will become significantly easier for those with the means.

On that point – both regarding health and cities – what do you think is driving these changes? Is it a fear of climate change and the realisation that we must adapt, or is it simply that new technology allows us to live longer and better? What creative opportunities will it present? What role does technology play here?

When it comes to cities, the big driver is the electrification of everything. This shift enables us to use entirely different vehicles than before. We previously relied on the same archetypal designs because that was the only viable option. Now, with new technologies making electrification more economical, we're not just seeing different solutions but significantly better ones.

This benefits not only the individual user but also the entire urban ecosystem. Technology enables cities to evolve, with e-bikes, lightweight two-, three-, and four-wheeled vehicles, and more efficient delivery systems transforming urban mobility. That's a massive change. But there's still a significant issue regarding travel that needs to be addressed.

What creative or technological opportunities does the future hold? What excites you the most?

Hopefully, in the next six to seven years, we'll see a dramatic shift in travel, making it more climate-friendly. The current approach – using sustainable aviation fuel (SAF) – isn't enough. It doesn't fundamentally change the energy profile of flight.

The real breakthrough will come from rethinking the aircraft itself, and that's where JetZero – a company in which I am an investor – comes in. JetZero is competing with Boeing and Airbus to develop the next generation of jets that use 50% less fuel while maintaining all the capabilities of today's aircraft – same engines, same fuel, same speed, same passenger and cargo capacity, and compatibility with existing airports. Considering that air traffic is expected to double or triple in the coming decades, solutions like JetZero are essential.

=="In the next six to seven years, we'll see a dramatic shift in travel, making it more climate-friendly."==

So, do you think the reality is that how we travel won't change dramatically? Will I still take the train to Heathrow or London City Airport, then board a similarly designed plane – just a more efficient one? Or do you see the travel experience itself evolving significantly?

There will be multiple shifts. First, the planes we use for long-distance travel will look completely different from today's aircraft. That's the only way we'll reach the efficiency levels we need.

But the most significant transformation will be in short-distance travel. We won't see nearly as many short-haul flights – there will be a massive shift towards rail. It's already happening globally, and even the United States is finally progressing on train infrastructure. Rail travel is much more efficient in every way.

I don't believe in air taxis and eVTOLs (electric vertical take-off and landing vehicles) as disruptions to urban transport – they're just alternatives to helicopters, not taxis. However, fully autonomous cars will expand beyond urban mobility to longer-distance travel.

==Urban transport will also evolve towards more point-to-point solutions, such as modular pods== – aerial, cable systems, or ground-based. These ideas have been floating around since the 1950s, but they're finally becoming feasible because they're highly efficient and remove street congestion.

When speaking with your peers about investing in these technologies or companies, what criteria do you look for?

The priority is solving pain points within existing systems. Jumping straight to entirely new systems is extremely difficult – unless it's in a place like a small city, an emirate, or a state with a top-down governance model that can implement change. ==In most democracies, the layers of permitting and regulation make it incredibly hard to get radical new ideas off the ground.==

For major transformations to happen, you often need a 'benevolent dictator' – a leader or governing body that can make decisive changes and prove their economic viability. Only then do these ideas gain traction.

That's why I focus on investments that improve existing infrastructure rather than trying to build entirely new systems from scratch. For example, investing in next-generation aircraft makes sense because they fit into the same airports, use the same fuel, and operate within current logistics networks – but with drastically better efficiency. That kind of innovation is far more likely to scale successfully.

Professionally speaking, how do you define your guiding principles?

Early on, I was just making technology for technology's sake. But over time, I realised that the real goal is to create solutions – what I call 'painkillers'. It's not just about cool technology, it's about understanding who it's for and how it can solve a problem. Ideally, those painkillers should feel like superpowers to the people using them.

That shift was a big moment for me – moving from just making things to solving real, immediate, or soon-to-be urgent problems. I'm not the guy thinking fifteen years ahead about how to fly to Mars – that's a whole different game. My focus has always been on practical, grounded, real-world solutions that still have an emotional and aesthetic appeal. ==The goal is to create things that change everyday life in an unexpected but deeply needed way.==

When do you think that mindset shifted for you? Because looking at your career, many of the things you developed require a level of foresight. The iPod, for instance, was unimaginable to most people before it existed. You must have had to think at least fifteen years ahead.

Funnily enough, this past weekend was the 35th reunion of General Magic, the company where we were essentially creating the iPhone – fifteen years too early. We were also working on AI-driven digital assistants – thirty-five years too early. That experience taught me a harsh lesson. The first decade of my career was filled with failure or, at best, middling success.

I learned that to create something truly impactful, you need the proper alignment of factors: the right technology, the right problem, and the proper social framework for people to adopt the change. Even the best idea won't take off if those stars don't align. That's why I stopped building things for fun – I wanted to create things that could make a positive impact.

I still think far into the future, but I've learned to work backwards. The future isn't just 10 or 20 years from now – it can be tomorrow. The key is plotting the steps to get there. Many people have great ideas about the future, but they don't think about how to bridge the gap from where we are today.

For me, the challenge is creating a roadmap – finding the stepping stones that keep the vision alive while making it achievable. It's never a perfect straight line because society and technology need time to evolve. But that's the skill I've refined: dreaming big while ensuring a clear and realistic path to get there.

For you, what's 'the next big thing' in your industry/field, and how might it impact our lives? How does it make you feel?

Right now, I often think back to 1999 to 2000, when people said, "The internet is going to replace everything in retail! Brick-and-mortar stores are dead! Everything will be delivered!" But that's not what happened.

Today, people say, "AI will take over the world! No one will have jobs!" But again, that's not how this plays out. It's about balance – understanding that technological revolutions come in waves. I've lived through so many: the personal computer wave, productivity and entertainment software, networking, communications, the rise of the internet, and then mobile, which transformed everything.

Each wave follows a pattern: initial hype, a trough of disillusionment, and then the real, long-term breakthroughs emerge. The most transformative internet companies didn't fully form until 2003–2004 – look at Google. Right now, I'm focused on what comes after this AI hype phase. What are the actual, substantial companies that will grow from it? Not just the noise but the lasting innovations. What we're hearing now is just hype – not all of it, but a significant amount.

What advice would you give to someone trying to navigate this?

Start with pain. Where's the pain? Where's the pain people have simply gotten used to and no longer question? That's where the opportunity is.

Instead of just envisioning some big, abstract idea, start by identifying the real pain points people face today. Then, project forwards – imagine a better world where those pain points are eliminated. That's your roadmap. Too many people start with a vision but have no idea how to get there.

If you start solving pain, you can weave that solution into a bigger vision. And you need milestones along the way. You can't spend years working on something in isolation before launching – it doesn't work like that anymore, and honestly, it didn't even work twenty years ago. You have to ship, get feedback, and iterate.

==“To create something truly impactful, you need the proper alignment of factors: the right technology, the right problem, and the proper social framework for people to adopt the change … That's why I stopped building things for fun – I wanted to create things that could make a positive impact.”==

You seem to push for meaning in your work. I'm thinking about how we live today – so much consumption, especially on our phones, and an overwhelming flood of content, a lot of it terrible. Have humans ever been exposed to so much junk at such a high rate?

There were plenty of times in my career when I could have gone for the quick buck – when I could have designed technology to manipulate people, to reprogramme them into behaviours that served my interests. But at the end of the day, it comes down to what kind of world you want to leave behind. Karma – it always comes back to you in some way.

It must be tricky always to do the right thing when your work is shaping the future?

I've always tried to take the high road. That's a personal choice. Others are purely motivated by making money, but I want to be able to look my kids and grandkids in the eyes and know I built something meaningful. I want future generations to say, "He wasn't perfect, but he tried to do the right thing."

I remember when we expanded iTunes from just music to TV and movies. In a meeting, someone suggested, "Hey, Steve, we should do porn – it would make a ton of money." Steve Jobs didn't hesitate. He said, "Sure, we could cash in. But is that the world we want our kids and grandkids to live in? Is that what we want to put our brand on? No way. Over my dead body."

People with a vision – who can implement change – are responsible for shaping the world they want to live in. And that vision evolves, especially when you have kids. Many young entrepreneurs don't think about the long-term impact of what they create because they're still focused on their independence and their journey. But it's often too late when they realise what they've built is causing social harm.

Finally, people talk a lot these days about how AI will make things easier. But setting AI aside, I want to ask about something more profound – your philosophy on hard work. What does it mean to you?

Hard work is the only way you truly learn. But it's not just about grinding – it's about working smart. You must push through failure because that's how you gain real experience. That's how you develop an understanding of what you're trying to accomplish.

No matter how advanced AI becomes or how much knowledge is available at your fingertips, you still have to work with people at the end of the day. You have to build things and make things happen. The world isn't just made of bits – it's made of atoms, and humans are in the loop.

You can read every management book out there – even mine – but you don't know what it takes until you're in the trenches, making decisions without a safety net. You have to work hard to push through uncertainty, to then develop mastery. And when you're staring at risk, with no precise data guaranteeing success, that's when real experience and confidence matter. Because in the end, there's no such thing as a sure bet – you have to work through enough challenges to trust your judgment when the time comes.

> "Hard work is the only way you truly learn. But it's not just about grinding – it's about working smart. You must push through failure because that's how you gain real experience."

Tina Fordham

Fordham advises CEOs, government leaders, and investors on how global instability will affect the world's economy and power structures. A pioneer in geopolitical foresight, she's helped major institutions prepare for the unpredictable. Her work sits at the intersection of politics, strategy, and ethics – exactly where future decision-making now needs the most clarity.

GEOPOLITICAL STRATEGIST & FOUNDER OF FORDHAM GLOBAL FORESIGHT

For twenty-five years, Tina Fordham has operated at the intersection of geopolitics and business, advising institutional investors, corporate boards, and executives on how global events shape the market environment. An early pioneer in the global foresight space, her career began in Eastern Europe after the fall of the Berlin Wall where she worked on democratic development and political reform initiatives in the former Soviet Union. Today, Fordham briefs influential parties worldwide, helping them navigate a geopolitical landscape that has fundamentally changed, with risks coming not only from emerging markets but also from Washington and Europe.

Fordham coined the concept of a 'geopolitical risk supercycle' to describe today's relentless instability, a trend now backed by data. An unprecedented cascade of crises, from trade wars to pandemics to armed conflicts, is straining the guard rails that once buffered global stability. Diplomacy is faltering and U.S.-led institutions are eroding, leaving leaders to face more frequent shocks with fewer safety nets. Fordham's mission is to instil foresight and agility in its clients, emphasising resilience and adaptation as strategic imperatives in this supercycle of disruption.

While hard power increasingly dominates global headlines, Fordham hasn't lost sight of soft power either. She cautions that cultural influence cannot be mandated and must grow organically, though turmoil often sparks creative renewal. She is also clear-eyed about technology's disruptions. Fordham warns that AI breakthroughs, while promising, could fray society if mismanaged. With automation poised to hit white-collar jobs – and a growing gap between fast-moving tech and slower-moving governance – she urges a pragmatic, ethical approach to innovation.

To start, please tell us a bit about your background and line of work, and where foresight fits into it. It sounds like that's a significant part of what you do.

I've been advising institutional investors, corporate boards, and the C-suite about the intersection of geopolitics and the business environment for twenty-five years, and I was one of the first people ever to do this. I started my career not in finance but working in Eastern Europe and the former Soviet Union after the Berlin Wall fell. Over time, I developed ways to combine political science and international relations with market analysis. Since I started, the demand for this kind of insight has only increased. Early on, I mainly talked about business opportunities in emerging markets and geopolitical risks abroad. But now we're seeing geopolitical risks coming from Washington and Europe. The whole landscape has changed. I started my firm three years ago, right after Putin's full-scale invasion of Ukraine, because I felt everything had changed – and I think that was the right call.

Even in such a short time, a lot has changed – broadly, do you see geopolitical instability accelerating now compared to three years ago?

Yes, absolutely. About two years ago, I published a piece outlining what I called a 'geopolitical risk supercycle'. In it, I posited that the rate and impact of geopolitical developments had increased markedly over the past decade, and we've since done empirical research that substantiates this. So yes, we are in the midst of a geopolitical supercycle. It's a term I borrowed from astronomy (relating to expansion), and one element of this hypothesis is that the guard rails that used to buffer these shocks are now weakening. Diplomacy is one example: we've seen diplomatic efforts struggling just recently. Another is the change in the United States' commitment to international institutions, which has been a pillar of globalisation and growth for the last 70 odd years. Our supercycle thesis is being actively tested, and so far it's confirmed that this isn't just a noisy news cycle – it's real. We're seeing measurable increases in every kind of geopolitical risk event, from tariffs and sanctions to conflicts and cyber attacks.

"You have to challenge what we call 'normalcy bias' – the assumption that things will continue as they always have – and confirmation bias, which is collecting only the information that supports what you want to believe."

Looking fifteen years into the future, what do you think these shifts will mean? Many people in Europe are used to a certain order, but you've noted that new blocs are forming. If we consider a fifteen-year horizon, do you see a new world order taking shape, new alliances or power structures we should anticipate?

Well, first of all, none of this is coming out of nowhere – it's been building for some time. I realise I use a different vocabulary with my international relations background, but let me summarise: the international order's shape is changing. It seems to be splitting into two camps: those countries that still believe in a rules-based system, and those that want to rewrite the rules to suit national interests. Our last briefing on this was actually titled 'A Tripartite World', referring to the U.S., China, and Russia, which is basically a return to a nineteenth-century model of regional hegemons. Now, what does that mean for everyone else? It means materials and resources might be harder to come by; supply chains could shorten. The free flow of ideas we've enjoyed may be more constrained. In general, the world could shrink to an extent. And if you happen to live in a borderland region or a piece of territory that one of these great powers wants, you might find yourself in a very tough situation. Now, this outcome isn't a foregone conclusion. I emphasise to the boards and executives I advise that during the Pax Americana – the post-Cold War order – people in business didn't have to spend much time worrying about geopolitics. They assumed they could fly anywhere, operate anywhere, and globalisation would just continue. Whether because of COVID or trade wars or other tensions, that assumption no longer holds. Going forwards, business leaders are likely going to have to engage much more in political considerations, both local and global. It used to be a luxury to say, "I'm not interested in politics", but that's not really viable now. If you don't like how things are going, you can protest or get involved, but you can't just ignore the political environment.

Do you think we're heading into a period where conflict is almost accepted as the norm? I mean, when you hear talk of a U.S. president wanting to buy Greenland or see Russia outright invading a neighbour, things that once seemed unthinkable are now happening. Are we looking at a future where major powers will just take what they want, and the world has to live with that?

We need to look at it in historical terms. The period from 1989, when the Berlin Wall fell, until 2007 (just before the global financial crisis) was the most peaceful and prosperous era in all of human history. So of course anything outside that window is going to feel more disruptive and unsettling by comparison. Yes, I do think we need to be prepared for more volatility and conflict than we became used to. We also should remember that roughly 85% of all wars throughout history have been over territory. So it's a bit naïve to ask, "Why would anyone go to war over a patch of land?" – because that's exactly what nations have always done. I think being good students of history will help us be better mentally prepared for what is likely to be a more complex environment. Greater awareness of these historical patterns will help anyone thinking about the future. In short, the world ahead probably won't look like that stable 1989–2007 period, and we have to adjust to that reality.

> "The future likely belongs to politicians who can form a direct connection with people, often through media like television or social platforms."

Many business leaders are trying to stay optimistic and find opportunities despite these tensions. Realistically, what are you saying to European business leaders about planning for the future in this climate?

I always remind them there's what a CEO says in public and then what they acknowledge in the boardroom. Europe right now is caught in the crosshairs between the U.S., China, and Russia, and we're really feeling it. Take the automotive industry: it's a sector heavily exposed to tariffs, reliant on tech, and tied to consumer confidence, so it's very sensitive to these geopolitical headwinds. I suspect in Europe we'll see intense debate about how much to align with China versus the U.S. – in other words, who is the more trustworthy partner. That's quite new. In the UK, for instance, there was a notion of 'cakeism' (having our cake and eating it too) – trying not to choose sides between China and the U.S. But now, with trade disputes heating up, industries like the automotive sector could get caught in the crossfire if a real trade war erupts. I'll tell you, I've never been as busy as I am now in my twenty-five years of doing this. CEOs and boards suddenly have to think about risks – like allies imposing tariffs on each other – that simply weren't on their radar before.

Let's talk about technology for a moment. How do you see the impact of breakthroughs like AI on this geopolitical landscape? We're experiencing incredible leaps in AI capabilities. Does this make it easier or harder to predict the future, and how are you advising leaders as our lives and economies become more digital?

As a practitioner, I do see a case for using large language models and big data analytics in our field. You can, for instance, comb through vast datasets for patterns. But all these tools are inherently backward-looking — they analyse the past to predict the future, which has limitations. We even experimented with AI in writing analysis, and it was a disaster; it produced boilerplate output. My team takes a very personal, tailored approach: we use data and historical analogues, but we also factor in a wide range of inputs and human judgment to project scenarios. That said, another critical aspect is how people react to AI in their lives. Companies clearly see that they can save a lot of money with AI — usually by laying off people. How will they do it? By automation, which means potentially significant job losses. That's where you see social risks: the strains on the social contract we've already seen in recent years are likely to get worse. There's a lot of money to be made with AI, but as with any revolutionary technology, it depends entirely on how it's applied. I also notice a gap between how businesses understand these tools and how governments do, which is concerning. Automation has already hit blue-collar jobs, next it will hit white-collar jobs, and that's a much trickier challenge for governments to handle. I wouldn't call myself a techno-optimist or a techno-pessimist, but rather a pragmatist. One consequence of the tech sector getting ahead of regulators is that the industry can push through its agenda, which might create problems for governments down the line.

> "Automation has already hit blue-collar jobs, next it will hit white-collar jobs, and that's a much trickier challenge for governments to handle."

You've spoken a lot about hard power dynamics. What about soft power? You were in the UK during the 'Cool Britannia' era of the 1990s, and we've recently seen South Korea expand its influence globally through K-pop, film, and culture. Can cultural soft power be wielded as effectively as military or economic power? And do countries need to get smarter about projecting a positive image abroad?

Yes, but soft power is tricky because you can't simply mandate creativity or culture. There has to be something organic about it. Often, times of turmoil lead to explosions of creativity – that certainly happened in the UK in the '90s. But you can't force it top-down. One of my favourite sayings about AI, for instance, is: "I don't need AI to write my poetry or do my art. I need AI to clean my house so I have time to do creative things." In other words, ==let technology handle the mundane tasks; human creativity is irreplaceable.== I do have some reservations on this front because if governments cut support for culture, it can stifle even organic creativity, and it might take time to recover from that. Still, history shows that even amid conflict and upheaval, you often get great art and cultural movements. So yes, soft power will continue to matter, but it's not something a government can entirely control – it's as much about people and their authentic creative output as it is about strategy.

What kind of leaders do you think will dominate in, say, fifteen years? We often watch world leaders gather and perform on the global stage, and it's clear some have mastered media better than others. Are future politicians going to be more like Trump – populist showmen – or do you see a different model emerging?

I think Donald Trump showed the importance of being a 'retail politician', someone who connects directly with the public. Even in a disastrous press conference, he blurted out, "This is going to make great TV." That tells you a lot. The future likely belongs to politicians who can form a direct connection with people, often through media like television or social platforms. And that can apply to politicians of any ideology. We already see that those who come across well on, say, TikTok or Instagram tend to perform better at the polls. Very few traditional politicians have figured that out yet.

Does that mean stoking fear and outrage is the winning formula? Social media tends to reward content that provokes anger or strong emotions – a lot of what goes viral is what stirs people up. Are the most successful future politicians going to be the ones who play on those emotions and divisions?

The politics of outrage certainly generates clicks and headlines, but there's always the risk of a backlash. ==I'm not convinced that perpetual outrage will win in the end.== I like to believe voters have agency and can choose not to remain in a state of fury. There's definitely a segment of politicians who thrive on fear-mongering, but I suspect there will also be a counter-movement of people who tire of that. So the jury is out. We might actually see that after a while, enough people say, "We want solutions, not constant anger", and those leaders who only stir the pot could face diminishing returns.

Amid all this, are there any bright spots you see around the world? Regions or markets that give you optimism? For instance, some of us feel that a decade ago there was a lot of optimism about places like Southeast Asia or China – it felt very open and full of opportunity. Nowadays, I hear more about the United Arab Emirates being a place where things get done and there's growth and stability. Outside the usual hubs like the U.S. or Western Europe, where do you see potential for businesses and investors?

It really depends on the sector. For services like finance and law, the Gulf cities in the Middle East are booming – we have clients expanding operations in places like Dubai and Riyadh. There is also some retraction from China in certain industries, due to geopolitical and regulatory concerns. That said, it's always been the case that certain markets become more attractive while others wane. What remains constant are a few fundamentals: political stability and rule of law. Those are non-negotiable for business. In that sense, Europe (and the UK) still have a lot going for them because, for all the challenges, they provide a stable, rules-based environment. Sure, incentives like tax breaks are nice icing on the cake, but they can't compensate for instability. So, it's not all doom and gloom for Europe or other developed markets. And yes, places like the Middle East are capitalising on a moment – they are offering stability, capital, and a welcoming business climate, which is attractive right now.

Finally, what core principles guide you in your work, and what do you advise leaders to keep in mind as they face the future?

First and foremost, be rigorous and analytical. You have to challenge what we call 'normalcy bias' – the assumption that things will continue as they always have – and confirmation bias, which is collecting only the information that supports what you want to believe. I push my clients to consider plausible alternative scenarios, even ones that are uncomfortable, rather than just assuming their preferred outcome will happen. We call it looking at 'plausible hypotheticals': basically, scenarios that have a reasonable chance of occurring, not just the scenario you hope for. Also, I pay a lot of attention to public opinion trends. Even authoritarian leaders have to care about public sentiment to some degree, because if they fail to deliver stability or prosperity, they can be removed (albeit in non-democratic ways). Lastly, remain open-minded. We have to constantly test our assumptions. Flexibility and willingness to question your own views are critical when navigating an uncertain future.

> "One of my favourite sayings about AI is: 'I don't need AI to write my poetry or do my art. I need AI to clean my house so I have time to do creative things.'"

Joe Gebbia

Gebbia co-founded Airbnb and helped it grow into a global platform that changed how people live, travel, and earn. With Samara, he's now focused on housing – designing adaptable homes for a shifting world. His work reflects a rare ability to turn ideas into systems that respond to real social and economic needs.

CO-FOUNDER OF
AIRBNB AND SAMARA

The story behind Airbnb has already gone down in Silicon Valley folklore: the two art school graduates struggling to pay their rent in San Francisco, noticing that a design conference would be bringing an influx of people to the city, and deciding to rent out Joe's air mattresses in their apartment to make a bit of extra money. The original name: AirBed & Breakfast. Today, it's the stuff of start-up legend.

Joe Gebbia was, along with current CEO Brian Chesky, one of the original co-founders. Having studied industrial design and graphic design at the prestigious Rhode Island School of Design (RISD), he was instrumental in ensuring that design was at the heart of the company right from the beginning. As he puts it: "For any consumer business, design is essential. If all else is equal between two products, the consumer is going to choose the one that's easier to use. And it's usually easier to use because it's been designed well."

Gebbia has always been heavily influenced by the twentieth-century industrial designers Charles and Ray Eames. This quote from Charles Eames, in particular, has been something of a lodestar for him throughout his career: "The role of the designer is that of a very good, thoughtful host, anticipating the needs of his guests." It's apt, given Airbnb now boasts a community of over 5 million 'hosts' of its own. With this ethos behind it, Gebbia's approach to design has always remained empathetic and highly user-centric.

In 2022, Gebbia stepped down from his operational role at Airbnb to focus on a variety of other projects and ventures. Chief among these ventures is Samara, a company that originally spun out of Airbnb, which builds and sells small, beautifully designed prefabricated houses. Its Backyard product, an accessory dwelling unit (or ADU), was honoured by *TIME* magazine as one of the 'best inventions of 2024'. Today, Gebbia is on a mission to grow the company within California; to expand Samara beyond the state; and more broadly to solve the widespread housing crisis in the United States.

Alongside Samara, Gebbia has also spent the past few years supporting purpose-driven companies and initiatives. For instance, in 2022, he joined the board of Tesla, and in 2023, donated $25 million to The Ocean Cleanup, a non-profit developing technologies to rid the world's oceans of plastic. He also founded the Eames Institute of Infinite Curiosity, an organisation dedicated to preserving the legacy of Charles and Ray Eames and teaching the next generation of designers and entrepreneurs the power of creative problem solving.

In this conversation, Gebbia discusses the power of design, the importance of tenacity, how he's attempting to rethink the housing market and the return of supersonic flight.

Professionally speaking, how do you define your guiding principles?

A professor at RISD once said to me: "Art raises questions, design answers them." **The guiding principle is: use design to solve problems.** Design is just a way of looking at the world, a thought process, and it gives you a lens that is very user-focused, where you're solving a problem by putting yourself in the shoes of the person you're designing for. Then you combine those insights with your own vision to create something new. Across everything I've done, the question has been: how do you design things that connect with people, can solve a problem for them, that are beautifully designed, that are easy to use, and that remove friction? Good design makes things enjoyable to use.

You've spoken in the past about how Charles and Ray Eames have influenced your approach as a designer. Which aspects of their work have most connected with you?

Everyone deserves good design, which is the Eames ethos. They showed that design is more than just how things look, it's how something works. They applied that across architecture, exhibition design, textiles, photography, films, products, and furniture. They were one of the first design studios to show the breadth of design, working horizontally across the world, and applying design to a variety of different mediums. The Eameses were some of the most prominent hybrid designers, which is very important for today. If you think about how consumers use products today, especially digital products, it's not just a mobile product or a desktop product or a web product. People are moving through different modalities as they experience a service. So it requires a hybrid approach to design.

Something else that the Eameses did, which I've fully embraced, is this idea of working backwards from the outcome that you want to create. So what do you envision as the ideal outcome of whatever problem you're trying to solve? Start there and then work backwards. Reverse engineer it. We do this at Samara – we start with the end in mind and work backwards. One of our values is literally called Work Backwards. We start by asking: "What's the ideal outcome?" We clearly articulate our answer. We optimise for that outcome, and reverse engineer the milestones to get there.

> "For the world to evolve and for things to be better designed, it takes the courage of designers to fight and push through the resistance, the rejection, and the noes that inevitably come up when you do something new."

You once wrote that one of the most important qualities guiding your entrepreneurship is 'diligence'. Can you talk us through what that means to you and how important it is?

There are a lot of words for diligence: hustle, grit, tenacity. They reflect the quality of the discipline that somebody has to push through. When you're trying to bring an idea to life as an entrepreneur or as a designer, there's going to be resistance. There are going to be people who say no. All the things around us that have been designed and produced are because somebody pushed through those noes. I can only imagine how many noes Benoît and Ressence got when they were trying to create the company, all the people who said, "No, you can't put oil in the watch face, that's crazy, that's never going to work." So, the fact that Ressence exists is a living, breathing example of determination, grit, hustle, tenacity, and willpower. Benoît knew he had to create the company, because there's always 1,000 reasons not to, and there's 1,000 people who will get in your way. It takes the courage of designers to fight and push through the resistance, the rejection, and the noes that inevitably come up when you do something new.

Let's talk about your latest venture, Samara, which is rethinking housing. Talk us through what you and your team are trying to do there.

The big mission for Samara is: how do we imagine people will live in the future, and how do we design products that guide us there? It takes too long to build housing right now in the United States. It's just too slow and there's a backlog of over 3 million homes that need to be built but can't, because it takes too long. So, what if it didn't? What if there were ways that we could create high-quality, beautifully designed homes that could be created in a fraction of the time, using hundred-year-old Model T methods of assembly lines and all the benefits of scale, instead of building a one-off house every time? This has been tried many times before, we're certainly not the first. But we've figured out the sweet spot of what a customer wants, what we can do in a factory, what design standards we're going to hold ourselves to from a quality standpoint, and what's economically feasible.

In California, which is our current market, we're doing really well, because California has a housing shortage and traditional construction is too slow. We've been able to enter the housing market through something called an accessory dwelling unit, or ADU, which is a backyard home. Anyone who lives outside California might never have heard of this acronym before, but in California, you either have one or you know someone who has one – one in five permits for a new home in California in 2023 were for an ADU. It's the fastest-growing segment of housing in the state. We have five different models, from a studio to what we call our XL 10, which is a two-bedroom, two-bath home. And in terms of construction, we're able to produce these in a fraction of the time. Governments love it because it can create more housing without putting up mid-rise apartment complexes that neighbours don't like. Neighbours love it because it's not changing the visual character of the neighbourhood. And homeowners love it because it creates this flex space to live your life – you can work out of a home office, you can house family, you can turn it into a rental property to earn income on demand. So it really becomes what the garage was in the 20th century, when it was for your car, but it was also more than that – it was your wood shop, then it was for band practice, then it was where the start-up was launched. And then you converted it into a tiny apartment. ==The ADU is the flex space of the twenty-first century.==

==*"The big mission for Samara is: how do we imagine people will live in the future, and design products that guide us there?"*==

Talk us through the design of these ADUs. How are you building the home of the future?

In terms of energy efficiency, it uses two times less energy than traditional construction with the same footprint. It's all electric and runs off solar panels on the roof. In fact, because it's so energy efficient inside, it actually generates more energy than it uses from the solar panels and we can send that energy into the main house. You effectively have a mini power plant in the backyard. Also, wildfires are a pretty devastating part of the state and so we designed it from the very beginning to be wildfire resistant. It has a standing seam metal roof and our siding options are metal or fibreboard, which are both fire resistant. We've designed for California in the future and what we know is top of mind for consumers.

We also handle everything for the customer. When they order online, they can customise a few things then hit order, and we handle everything else from there. Imagine if you ordered an iPhone off Apple's website and it came in a bunch of different pieces and required a bunch of other people to come and put it together. No one would order an iPhone, it would be ridiculous. We've taken that same approach to your home. You configure online, just like a phone, and we do a bunch of things at the same time. We handle the permitting, the surveying, utility hook-ups, and the foundation, which all takes about four weeks in the backyard. Simultaneously, we're in the factory starting to produce your home, which also takes about 30 to 60 days. So we can expedite this entire process, and within just a couple of months, we ship a fully finished home on our truck. It shows up at your house and we crane it onto our foundation. The whole process takes about two hours, and it's done. This is what the future of construction could look like.

Joe Gebbia

For you, what's 'the next big thing' in your field, and how might it impact our lives? How does it make you feel?

In the housing context, the next big thing is designing for infill. In California, they've passed laws that allow you to take a single family home lot, which previously would only allow you one home, and maximise that land with a variety of different structures: single family homes, ADUs, duplexes. The way that Samara is approaching it is, of course, through a design lens. So we're not going to jam everything together, it's not going to be some horrific-looking, 'maximise every square foot' configuration. We have this whole family of products that we can configure in an infinite number of ways to now do infill in a really strategic, beautiful way. Imagine what happens when we apply our process from small to 'full size' homes.

What creative opportunities will it present?

In the future, you'll see single family home lots viewed very differently from how they have been in the past, where they'll be effectively rezoned or re-permitted in ways that allow for really creative and thoughtful infill development. We're in pole position to help bring twenty-first century ideas around design, production, systems, and methodologies to an industry that very much operates out of the twentieth century. Hopefully that solves one of the biggest problems, which is just the speed of construction. We are accelerating the speed with which homes are made in the United States, starting in California, but over time we'll expand far beyond California. We'll be able to reach people with fast-built homes at a reasonable price that are beautifully designed. And hopefully make the Eameses proud.

Generally speaking, what creative opportunities does the future hold? What are you particularly excited about?

Supersonic flight. It's coming back through Boom Supersonic. I'm very excited about this company; I got to invest in them years ago, and they're really at the forefront of bringing back this technology that, of course, existed before with the Concorde, but never really had the right economic model to be sustainable. Boom is crushing it. They just had their first successful test flight, with their new engine achieving supersonic speeds. It is actually the first privately flown supersonic flight ever. They've already got pre-orders from United and Japan Airlines, and a couple other airlines, but it will radically change the speed with which people travel. So, New York to Paris is eight hours; it would now be four hours. LA to Sydney is eighteen hours; now, nine hours.

Anything else that you're excited about?

==Something I think about all the time is how the value of offline experiences is always going up.== That's why I'm so excited about the Eames Institute of Infinite Curiosity and what we're building in Petaluma, California, at the Eames Ranch. It's going to facilitate some of the most incredible experiences. It's the place to go to experience the lives of Charles and Ray Eames, and to experience their lessons and the work that they left behind through the prototypes, the artefacts, the films — we have the entire collection of everything, it's close to 60,000 objects. And so we can tell the story of their legacy and their lessons through the things they left behind and make it very experiential for people. And to me, the value of that's only going to go up in the future. When you connect the next generation of entrepreneurs, designers, and thinkers to the age-old lessons of Charles and Ray Eames — through these offline experiences that are tactile, rich, immersive, and memorable — we can help open up people's minds to the role of design and creativity, and solve some of the world's biggest problems.

Lonneke Gordijn

CO-FOUNDER OF STUDIO DRIFT

Co-founder of Studio DRIFT, artist Lonneke Gordijn creates large-scale installations merging nature, technology, and emotion. Her projects – such as drone performances and kinetic sculptures – redefine how we experience public art. Her visionary perspective explores technology's role in forging deeper human connections, offering an essential view on art's role in future societies.

Since founding Studio DRIFT in Amsterdam in 2007 alongside Ralph Nauta, Lonneke Gordijn has pioneered work showcasing how art, technology, and nature can meaningfully come together. Studio DRIFT's installations – always displayed in artful motion – combine a sophisticated approach to engineering with a distinct human sensitivity that captivates audiences worldwide. From sending thousands of crowd-dazzling, birdlike synchronised drones into the skies above Art Basel Miami Beach to suspending luminous dandelions in miniature glass domes to symbolise the fragility of life, the studio's work challenges our perceptions of both the artificial and natural worlds.

In an era where technology seems to be isolating us from each other, Gordijn's work with Studio DRIFT attempts to do the opposite, using innovation to unite, inspire, and even reshape our collective future. It's a bold ambition, but the artist argues that collective action for the good of humankind requires emotional engagement – not just theoretical understanding. Her installations aim to bridge this gap, turning the abstract into the tangible. For example, *Drifters* animates concrete blocks to evoke empathy towards the built environment – connecting audiences with the building industry's detrimental impact on the planet.

For Gordijn, time has taken on heightened significance, particularly after becoming a mother. She strongly advocates presence, urging mindfulness about how we spend each moment. This clarity influences her creative decisions, underscoring Studio DRIFT's emphasis on meaningful, timeless interactions rather than fleeting digital distractions. "It's about spending time in the right way", she reflects – an ethos directly translating into artworks that demand genuine attention and contemplation. Lonneke Gordijn's vision offers a compelling, hopeful future defined by harmony between technology, nature, and humanity. Studio DRIFT's work is a powerful argument for innovation that truly serves human connection.

Studio DRIFT's work has been at the intersection of art and technology since 2007. Did you foresee that technology would increasingly have a bigger impact on our lives moving forwards when you started your practice?

No, not at all. It was not planned. It came from our natural interests, and then learning from the ideas that we had, we had to get to know a lot of technology. We were not educated as engineers or technologists, but we discovered many things in this sphere by doing our work. Our work doesn't come from the mindset, "Hey, we have this technology and what can we do with it? Let's make a surface or an app or something." Our work comes from what we want to experience. Our work is always very close to us as artists and technological aspects have become necessary.

Today, it's interesting since we see a lot of technology around us, and we're thinking, "Hey, where is the human aspect? Where's the human centre?" It became our interest, this intertwinement of working with engineers and talking about translating emotions into data and output. Asking: "How can you make an engine work in a way that speaks to us humans in an emotional way?" We're talking about two different languages here. How do you make sense of these things? How do they become useful for humans?

Not that long ago, social media had a level of social engagement, and when Facebook started, you were actively encouraged to be part of the conversation. Now, Instagram and TikTok don't prioritise true social action. We're being spoon-fed content by an algorithm, and these companies have weirdly stripped the 'social' from 'social' media. Is technology stripping humanity out of the way we live these days?

We are so addicted to these technologies because we – as humans – need to respond to our environment. Everything that moves attracts our attention immediately – that is our survival mechanism, this is who we are – and social media is moving based on videos. So it just takes us – we're absorbed by it. There is some sense of humanism in how we respond to it, why we are so into it and addicted to it, and our need for togetherness, safety, the group, and survival. Where do I fit in? This is a massive question for humans, and social media steps in to answer this question, but not in a fulfilling way. Ultimately, it helps fulfil parts of our needs, but despite making us think we're more connected, it's making us more disconnected.

How would you say your work brings people together around technology?

It's one big process. It's not so much about technology as it is about movement. We make our artwork move so that it becomes something people want to respond to. It can be a rhythm; naturally, the audience will start breathing to the rhythm, and heartbeats align with it.

You can use movement deliberately and tune people to the same wavelength, and being on the same wavelength is important for connecting. That brings connection and understanding and gives everyone the same energy. We naturally seek these moments. This happens at dance parties, during a football match, or when you have a good connection with someone; the chemistry goes back and forth. Because you're on the same wavelength, you completely understand each other. That enlightens and lifts us, especially with a bigger group; it feels great. You're energised. If you have entirely different energies in a room, and nobody tries to align, those energies fight each other, draining everyone.

I learned all this from making our artwork. I wasn't looking for it deliberately, but I was always looking for floating forms of being that I didn't feel in my daily life, because there was too much stress and things going on, but these were the feelings I longed for. ==When you experience something great, you want someone else you like to also experience it.== So, our work came through a need to look at what's happening to other people and myself, and why these artworks feel this way. Now that I know this, I have started to look into the science around it. There are studies about this, and we have begun to use it more deliberately. We use these rhythms and movements and we reprogramme them so that they speak to us, and then it's more like choreography, like a ballet, but then it's more of a story. It depends on what we use in the artwork, and how we can establish the best connection between people and the artwork, and people amongst themselves.

> "You can use movement deliberately and tune people to the same wavelength, and being on the same wavelength is important for connecting."

What creative/technological opportunities does the future hold? What are you particularly excited about?

The type of technology is not relevant to me. What matters more is what we want to achieve with it. I like to work from that. **I want to use technology to create togetherness.** Through it, we create awareness and connect with people. Back in the day, there was the church, which had a specific function that is not embedded in many Western societies anymore. While the church's influence has lessened, there is still the need for us as people to feel part of a group and be empowered by connectedness.

If you were doing this interview with Ralph Nauta, my partner in crime at Studio DRIFT, he would say he's excited by AI. Yes, we are exploring this as a studio, but I see AI more as something that can help in the work process to make things easier or to develop things more easily, or even to build software. So it saves time. That is important. Time is of the essence, and that's what we lack the most. We need to use time in a valuable way.

In what sense do you think about time and use time? How does this help you define your guiding principles?

I had a son nine months ago, and the way I use my time has drastically changed because I have to take care of him. Now, I get very impatient with things that take too long or are unnecessary. It makes my focus very clear. I think about the years before his birth when I was rushing, working – completely absorbed in my mind. And then, wow, after having a child, I am so much more connected. Having two feet in this world with everyone else is much more important than being on my own little planet.

With less time for myself, I'm much more creative now. It's funny, but it's true. So, what is valuable when it comes to time and my principles? It's about spending time in the right way, in every moment of your life. Some moments will never come back, so being present and aware of those special moments with certain people, like family and friends, is imperative. My advice is to be mindful that when you're having a good experience, enjoy it in the moment instead of thinking afterwards: "Oh! I was quite happy then." It's better to realise it in the moment. Enjoy it.

Your work often examines significant issues we humans face, like climate change. Looking to the future, how can we positively confront these challenges?

What worries me now is decision-making and the lack of long-term vision. With our work, we study how to unite people, because I think the more separated we are – like how we are in the modern political landscape – the less we can do. We have to make decisions as a collective and stick to them and not constantly shift systems. That's sustainable thinking. Right now, we can talk about solutions for garbage and rising sea levels, but we're not making group decisions. We're not taking any steps collectively. We're just debating, and it drives me crazy. I find it such a waste of time, so I think we are on the wrong track. That's why I believe we have to look at nature for decision-making and systems.

We work against all the systems we build. We have created a world that's collapsing, which sounds quite negative. The positive side is that we have it in us, and it's in our nature to fight together, and that is what I believe. It's about a sustainable way of thinking and a bigger idea of how the world should function, and to which systems we should look for sustainability, because nature has already figured this out. I am positive about what humans can do – if we look together towards nature. It's up to us. It doesn't look so easy now, but it can be easy. So, we have a mission here as artists to promote the idea, knowledge, and system of uniting ourselves in one direction.

How do you tell timeless stories in your work and raise awareness that affects humanity in the long term?

Drifters is an installation about the built environment. With a floating concrete block as its symbol, we've made this element come alive and move through the air – as if it's weightless. It challenges the audience because we typically have no relationship with concrete blocks – we don't even think about these objects, even though they define so much of what is built around us.

By suddenly making a block of concrete move in a specific way, we establish an emotional connection with the audience in that installation, which is extremely weird. It is so weird to feel something for a concrete block because it should make no sense – but with *Drifters*, it does. When you feel something, you can act on that feeling. If you don't feel something, what you're examining becomes a theory, no matter how important the subject matter is. You rarely act on a theory – you might be made aware of it during the day, but afterwards, you go back home, eat dinner, watch your Netflix, and sleep – no real relationship is established.

==On important matters, we must work on solutions to transition from people feeling nothing to people feeling something.== Of course, making flying concrete blocks won't define the future – that's not the point. But ideas like this that establish more emotional human relationships with our built environment must proliferate.

==" We have a mission here as artists to promote the idea, knowledge, and system of uniting ourselves in one direction."==

You're opening a gigantic museum in Amsterdam this year, 2025. How will it help define the future?

This building is energy-positive – so from a sustainability standpoint, it gives back energy. It's a listed building from the late 1800s, completely redone with various inventions. During the pandemic, we realised how much artwork we ship worldwide for exhibitions, and it's very unsustainable. So, instead of repeating ourselves and spending a lot of money on shipping, we would rather spend that money on developing and showing artwork in the best possible way. We are almost 18 years old as a studio, and we already have artworks that are 10 years old and haven't been shown correctly as we didn't have the right environment to do so. But this new museum is the place where we're going to do these things.

We will develop an educational program here that shows positive pathways for the future and what humanity, technology, and nature are capable of. Many kids nowadays are apprehensive about the future, but we have many possibilities that empower kids as well as adults. It's imperative for us to inspire and to bring a certain mindset that creates trust and positive ideas about the future.

The opening show will include all our artworks across eighteen rooms filled with installations. Over time, we will collaborate with other artists, but it will always be about what's happening now. So we will work with artists with experiential works, but it depends on who is looking ahead to the future, which is very important. It's really about the present and the future instead of the past.

Christopher D. Harvey

PROFESSOR OF NEUROBIOLOGY AT HARVARD MEDICAL SCHOOL

Harvey's work at Harvard aims to decode cognition at the level of individual cells. Through custom optical tools and virtual reality, he exposes how decisions form in the brain. With implications across neuroscience, mental health, and machine intelligence, he's building foundational knowledge for how future thinking – human or artificial – will be understood and designed.

What makes us individuals? What does a thought look like in the brain? And when we're making a decision, what is actually going on at a molecular level? These are just some of the vast and complex questions that lie at the heart of Christopher D. Harvey's research. As Professor of Neurobiology at Harvard Medical School in Massachusetts, he runs the Harvey Lab, which investigates 'the neuroscience of navigation' – in other words, the brain functions that underpin how we make decisions while moving through space.

While Harvey's research has profound implications for our understanding of the human brain, it doesn't actually involve any humans at all. Instead, the vast majority of his experiments focus on mice, and training them to carry out decision-making tasks within maze-like virtual reality environments. Navigation might seem like a peculiar entry point into such monumental questions around cognition and intelligence, but Harvey explains that it is highly useful for testing the fundamentals. "We focus on navigation because it has a lot of aspects of reasoning and decision making, but it's more tractable in mice in a laboratory setting", he says. "But once we understand some of that, we can start to extrapolate to bigger questions."

The field of neuroscience, he tells us, has been growing rapidly over the past decade, powered by cutting-edge new technologies – from the use of light to stimulate neurons to the development of highly specialised microscopes to new and more accurate ways of measuring brain activity. The Harvey Lab has played a major role in developing and pioneering some of these, not least the use of VR environments for mice, which are now a 'bread-and-butter' element of almost all the lab's experiments. As Harvey himself puts it, "My research and technology development go hand in hand."

Looking to the future, Harvey is confident that the pace of development within his corner of neurobiology won't be slowing down any time soon. New technologies that are just coming online now will allow him and his colleagues to target and manipulate different types of cells within the brain, while other scientists are using special electron microscopes to create 'wiring maps' of the mouse brain. "That's going to be a huge revolution", says Harvey. Needless to say, he and his colleagues at the Harvey Lab will be at the forefront of that revolution.

In this conversation, we discuss how Harvey's interest in neuroscience was initially sparked, hear how technology has supercharged the field, and learn about the potentially profound implications his research could have on everything from mental health to artificial intelligence.

Professionally speaking, how would you define your guiding principles? What are the principles that you've lived by throughout your career?

I have a passion for discovery. If we know what the answer is going to look like, and we just have to do some work to get there, it's less interesting to me. I love it when we're going into the unknown and we don't know what the answer is – we don't even know what the answer is going to look like. Creativity is another. Everyone thinks that, in science, there's one way to do things and one answer that you're going to get out of it, but there's really an art form and a creativity to how you actually tackle a question. A question like: how does the brain work? If you asked 1,000 scientists to study this, they would do 1,000 different things and have different ideas. Building technology and creativity together towards discovery – that has really guided me and keeps me passionate about doing this, because there's always more to discover.

Our understanding of creativity can be so narrow, can't it? We think of it in the arts and design, but it's rare that creativity is acknowledged within the sciences.

Some of the best scientists are the most creative ones. They're really visionary and they see connections between things that others can't see. It's hard to teach, but I try to encourage my students to think about it. When I was first getting into science, I thought that you had a question and you would just do the experiment to test that and there would be one answer, and everyone would do it the same exact way. But actually there's a lot of creativity. There is creativity when you look at what others have discovered and done before, and then from that, pick out what you think are the most important points and connect all the dots. Everyone will connect them in different ways. How do you make those connections to develop a new idea? Then, when you design an experiment, there are a million different ways you could design an experiment, and creativity comes in asking: am I going to use this one type of experiment versus another? And then after you get the results, there's creativity in how you interpret them.

You spoke about when you started out in science. Take us back to the beginning of your academic studies. How did you first get interested in the field of neurobiology?

When I was doing my undergraduate work, I actually studied biomedical engineering, but I started to take some classes in biology and got really excited about the basic biology of how cells function, and what the different proteins and molecules are doing in cells. I did a bit of research as an undergraduate and fell in love with the hands-on aspect of doing experiments. And then when I went to graduate school, I actually thought I was going to tackle questions around cancer research, but one of my classmates told me about this cool emerging area of neuroscience. So, I worked in the neuroscience lab briefly and immediately fell in love with it, because it brings together all these different topics of how cells function and big topics about cognition and intelligence. I haven't looked back since.

What got you interested in the neurobiology of navigation, specifically? What was it about this area that really appealed to you at the beginning?

==Understanding the brain is really one of the big frontiers in science and still very little is known about some aspects of brain function.== What really stood out to me is that there are things that are really inherent to who we are as people and individuals, like how we reason, how we think, the decisions we make, things even as big as: who do we marry, what school do we go to, what career do we pursue? These are built from our genes, from the experiences we've had, all things that are really personal. But at the end of the day, they're all building from the cells and molecules in our brains, and how these cells connect to each other. You have these really small cells, they're all connected to each other, and then you get this amazing emergent property of thoughts and decisions and reasoning. How that happens is still a mystery. I don't think it's going to be solved in my lifetime.

Also, as we think about some of the more complex disorders and mental illnesses, like schizophrenia, bipolar disorder, and dementia, these are big issues in our societies and big issues for the individuals as well. Again, we don't know that much about the underlying causes. How do we help people with this? So, all those things got me inspired.

> "That's why I think the word 'frontier' is appropriate, because it is an unknown kind of darkness or wilderness that we're going into, and we have to figure things out."

Christopher D. Harvey

> "We're still in the very early days. But over the past ten years, there's been a crazy revolution in technology to measure and manipulate brain activity."

You used the word 'frontier'. How much or little do we really know about how the brain works? How would you describe our current understanding of the brain functions that underlie cognition, intelligence, and decision-making?

The field is in an exponential growth phase, where we're making major leaps in understanding. We don't know everything about it, but we're making really good progress in understanding how individual brain cells function, how they connect to each other, how they talk to each other, and how things dysfunction in some diseases. We're still in the early days, though, of how that all translates to intelligence or cognition. One of my colleagues was saying that those questions are like trying to put a man on the moon in the year 1800. We're still in the very early days. But over the past ten years, there's been a crazy revolution in technology to measure and manipulate brain activity. We can use light to stimulate neurons. We can measure the activity of large parts of the brain all at once. It's really transformed the types of data that we can collect and what we can potentially understand.

Given there's been this dramatic growth phase over the past decade or so, what's 'the next big thing' in your field? And how might it impact our lives, and society at large?

Two big themes that are really emerging in neuroscience at the moment are: how the body affects the brain, and also how social interactions affect the brain. Regarding the first one, people have thought for a very long time about how the brain controls the body. The brain controls our muscles, our heartbeats, all kinds of things. But there's a growing appreciation that there is a very close interaction between the two. There's been lots of work on how the gut microbiome, for example, can actually affect the brain, even in the realm of intelligence, cognition, reasoning, and thinking. That was underappreciated for a long time and is now emerging.

The other aspect of this is the social aspect. Social interactions are really critical – we all know that from our day-to-day lives. But looking at how those interactions then actually have a direct impact on all these processes of reasoning and the cells in the brain, that is still an emerging area of neurobiology. That's going to be another huge frontier.

How do you think about the long-term aims of your research?

The long-term aim is to take something that seems abstract, like making a decision, and break that down into all of the underlying biological building blocks. What are the individual molecules doing? What individual cells are doing things? What is the sequence over time by which these things transpire? How do these cells talk to each other? What parts of the brain are operating at different time points to create a decision? So, take things that are abstract and describe them from that level. That's my long-term goal.

One thing that strikes me is that your work has some really profound philosophical implications around the idea of free will. If there's a biology of decision-making, it will affect how we think about free will. Do you think about that kind of thing?

That's not something I think about too much. I agree, though, that my work definitely takes things that sound very abstract, human things, maybe even glorified things like reasoning and thinking, and it brings them down to the very nuts-and-bolts level of molecules and cells. But at the end of the day, that is where things emerge from. In my view, there's nothing magical. It's just the biology of it. Once we know more about the rules of it, we'll understand much more about what a thought actually is. What does a thought actually mean? So yes, it definitely does raise some of these philosophical questions.

And in the long term, what profound changes might your research enable, whether that's in the medical field or in the technology field or elsewhere?

Obviously one aspect of why we do this is to help with mental illnesses. The other side is artificial intelligence. A lot of AI has been inspired through neuroscience. Neural-network models are loosely inspired by what we know about neuroscience. Now the fields have diverged, because the AI field has gone off and is a little less inspired by neuroscience, and has become a big engineering, computer-science endeavour. But I think there are still things that the brain does much better than AIs. You think about creativity, flexibility, the ability to generalise from one scenario to another – AIs still struggle with that. There's still a gap between what AIs can do and what our brains can do, and we don't fully understand yet where that gap is coming from. So there's an opportunity that if we understand how the brain is doing that, we could inform new algorithms for AI that could enhance their capabilities to a whole new level. Another injection of insight from neuroscience could help with that.

Thinking about the potential future that you are helping to bring about, how does that make you feel on a personal level?

Whenever I think about the questions around understanding the basics of brain function, those are the things that get me out of bed in the morning. Those are the things that I can't stop thinking about at night, that I always come back to. That's where my passion and energy come from. We don't know what the answer is going to look like; we don't know how we're going to get there. It takes a lot of hard work to figure this out, but that's where the excitement is: going into the unknown, charting our own new path. That's why I think the word 'frontier' is appropriate, because it is an unknown kind of darkness or wilderness that we're going into, and we have to figure things out. That's very exciting.

Looking towards the future, what creative opportunities will your research reveal or create?

One of the things that I've thought about is what makes us individuals. We all have different genes. And we all have different experiences that form our memories. We know that those are aspects of who we are as individuals. But the next step of that, which I'm excited about, is how that foundation of genes and experiences then means, at any moment in time, that we can use that foundation to generate something new, generate a new action, a new decision. I really want to understand that. And I think that's really at the centre of us as individuals. So I think if we understand that much better, we'll also appreciate each other much more, what makes us similar and different. We'll be able to see each other's perspectives more.

Let's talk about technology. What role does technology play in your research?

Technology is a huge part of what we do. One thing that's really helped our research, and that I've been at the centre of developing, is virtual reality technology for mice. You can think of it as having mice play video games in VR, and we can then probe how they're making decisions and using their experiences. ==We use VR technology as a bread-and-butter tool for a lot of our experiments.== Then there is other science that we really build from. For instance, we design and build custom microscopes that we can use to look into the brains of mice as they're making decisions. And that gives us the opportunity to figure out and predict what mice are going to do. Other groups have developed electrodes that can measure the electrical activity of individual brain cells. There's also been a revolution in gene editing and viral technologies to change the genetics of mice, as a test of how that affects different aspects of brain function. Then there's this whole field of optogenetics, where we can now use light to stimulate groups of neurons in the brain. All of these things have come online in the past ten to fifteen years. So there's really been a technology-driven growth in neuroscience, where we have abilities to measure and manipulate brain function, and understand things about the gene expression in the brain both at a deeper level and on a broader scale than we've ever been able to do before. My research and technology development go hand in hand; we always need new technologies. They're always aiding our discoveries. And then with a new discovery, you realise you want to do something new, and then you have to develop new technology to achieve that.

Talk us through how VR for mice actually works. Do the mice have tiny headsets on?

Some people are now developing little headsets for mice. The way we do it, and the way we first developed it, the mice are surrounded by a large screen, like a huge IMAX screen, and then they run on top of a ball, which we call a spherical treadmill. We measure with optical sensors how that ball is rotating, and send those signals to a computer that updates the screen. So if they run forwards, we move them forwards in the VR; if they turn one way, it turns the VR. So they can run through these different mazes in the virtual environment, and we have them run down a simplified city block, making turns left and right based on landmarks and things like that.

Absolutely incredible. And lastly, generally speaking, what creative and technological opportunities does the future hold? What are you particularly excited about?

What makes us individuals? How do all these experiences and our genes come together to make us individuals? What does a thought look like in the brain? And when we have a thought, when we're making a decision, what is actually going on in the brain? If, at the end of my career, we've made some progress towards understanding those things, if we can write them down in a less abstract way than we can now, I'll feel like we've made great progress. And that's what I'm shooting for.

==

"There's still a gap between what AIs can do and what our brains can do, and we don't fully understand yet where that gap is coming from."

Masayuki Hirota

As Editor-in-Chief of Chronos Japan, Masayuki Hirota is a leading authority on watchmaking, deeply versed in both tradition and innovation. His sharp insights illuminate how craftsmanship, market shifts, and technology shape consumer preferences, making him ideally positioned to navigate the future evolution of independent brands and global watch culture.

EDITOR-IN-CHIEF AT CHRONOS JAPAN

Masayuki Hirota's love for watches began at an early age. "I got interested in watches when I was about twelve years old, after reading one of my father's books about wristwatches", he says. "After that, I bought my first watch, an antique Cyma watch, in an antique shop in Tokyo. From then on, I was fascinated." After a spell working for his father's small company, he decided at the age of thirty to resign and turn his hobby into a career, becoming a watch journalist.

Today, Hirota-san is the Editor-in-Chief of *Chronos Japan*, a media outlet established in 2004 that specialises in watches. In this role, he leads a small team of seven – five journalists, covering both print and web content, and two additional staff members – and closely follows the trends and broader shifts in the watch industry, both in Japan and globally. "We focus on very niche topics and structure each issue around a specific theme. I think that's the reason we're still surviving in this industry," says Hirota-san, referring to how important it is to find a strong USP in the modern media landscape.

Over the course of his 20-year career at *Chronos Japan* (he was the magazine's main contributor for twelve years before he became Editor-in-Chief), Hirota-san has seen the watch industry go through multiple transformations, from the COVID pandemic and the market boom that accompanied it, to the recent tilt from many collectors towards smaller brands and independent watchmakers. His grounding in the recent history of the sector also lends him a deeply informed perspective on where it might be going next. He believes that thanks to new technologies and collectors' changing tastes, we are currently witnessing a new era of creativity in the watch world, and it's one that is set to continue. "We are entering a new era," he says, "where true creative freedom is possible."

In this conversation with Hirota-san, we discuss how the watch world has changed over the past decade, how brands such as Ressence are reshaping the industry, and look ahead to what might be around the corner for brands and buyers alike.

Professionally speaking, how do you define your guiding principles? What are the consistent principles or values that have led you throughout your career?

In general, I always try to stay close to the mindset of the buyer and watch collectors. That's the most important point. Every time I look at watches, I try to keep the same mindset I'd have if I were considering buying one myself. I try to avoid judging watches solely on their price. Price is not the most important factor. While higher prices may increase the likelihood of a better finish, uniqueness and a cohesive package are fundamentally unrelated to cost. And lastly, I try not to let my personal collection and my personal tastes influence how I criticise other watches.

When you talk about your own collection, how would you describe your taste, your style?

Generally, I prefer conventional, slightly old-fashioned and old-school watches. That said, I've also come to appreciate modern, avant-garde, and provocative watches. Of course, as professionals, we have to clearly separate our personal preferences from our assessment of whether a watch is objectively good.

The watch industry went through quite a turbulent time during the COVID pandemic. Lots of people were stuck at home and had more disposable income; they got interested in watches, perhaps because you can admire them without leaving your house! You spoke just now about wanting to adopt the mindset of a collector. How do you feel buyers and collectors have changed since the pandemic? Are they looking for different things now?

I'm not sure if it's fortunate or unfortunate, but during the period of the COVID pandemic, the watch market really struggled (to keep up with demand), particularly the larger brands, and lots of newcomers joined the field. After that, I think the quality of the market has drastically increased. During COVID, many collectors satisfied their desire for more mainstream timepieces, like the Patek Philippe Nautilus or the Audemars Piguet Royal Oak. Fortunately, some collectors are now seriously looking for real watches, watches that are more personal and meaningful for themselves. It's a great change and good news for this industry. The market has become much more mature and this is a good opportunity for small watchmakers.

Another thing that supposedly happened during the pandemic was that some of the bigger brands noticed the higher demand and raised their prices, in some cases a lot, which angered collectors. Is that how you see it?

Yes, I agree with you. Some watchmakers were slightly greedy. It became a trigger for change in the market. For better or worse, the pandemic had a significant impact on the watch market, but the current situation is better than before. As a result, what we now see is that serious collectors remain – those who seek watches that excel in both quality and price. In other words, the enthusiasm that was once there for flashy Daytonas has, in some cases, led people to buy Ressence.

I remember going to watch events in the 2010s and independent watchmaking wasn't really thriving. The bigger brands were very dominant back then. Has that changed now?

That's right. There are a few reasons for this. One reason is that the watch market was slightly conservative and rigid in that time, but during the pandemic so many young and passionate collectors joined the field. That was the trigger for change. Lots of them were looking for very eminent watches like the Nautilus and Royal Oak, but others wanted watches that are much more scarce in the market. The number of such collectors is still relatively small, but it's enough to support the growing popularity of independent watchmakers. The market has matured. The result is the booming of independent watchmakers.

Why did so many independent brands start up during that time? Was it simply because there was so much new demand coming into the watch industry?

Now there are so many independent watchmakers. Two years ago, I talked with Maximilian Büsser (founder of watch brand MB&F) and he told me that, during the COVID era, many watchmakers and creators had to show their face for the first time in order to showcase their creations to collectors. He felt that shift helped lead to the rise in demand for small watchmakers, because collectors liked that they could see the face behind the product. They liked that the watchmaker was talking to them directly. And then, of course, with the expansion of the internet, watchmakers can now easily sell their watches directly to their customers. There is far less need for them to attend major watch events.

"The next ten years will be hard for certain smaller brands, because the market is so matured that collectors are really looking for a good all-round package."

Masayuki Hirota

> "Thanks to new technologies and the younger generation of talented, visionary watchmakers, innovation is accelerating. And in watchmaking, innovation is almost synonymous with creativity."

How does Ressence fit into this story?

I think Ressence is very important for this industry. This answer is going to be a bit technical. Mechanical watches have the advantage of delivering much stronger torque than quartz movements. Essentially, mechanical movements are much more powerful. This allows for thicker, longer hands and the power to drive complex mechanisms, like perpetual calendars and chronographs. This is the key to expanding the creative capabilities for ambitious new creators like Ressence. Now, recently, improvements in the torque control and escapements have enabled new possibilities for ultra-high-frequency pieces and much more complex timepieces, like the Jacob & Co. Astronomia Tourbillon, for instance. It has also opened a new field for brands like Ressence and Urwerk, which are great examples of the new era of mechanical watches. Thanks to the larger torque of mechanical movements and the wonderful control of the torque from the mainspring, Ressence is doing things that were impossible twenty years ago. It's very scarce but it's wonderful. Ressence has opened up new possibilities for mechanical watches and that's why it's very important.

For you, what's 'the next big thing' in the watch industry? What are you kind of expecting in the next few years that could transform the industry?

My opinion is quite simple. Thanks to advancements in machining technology, watch cases have become much more refined and three-dimensional. Richard Mille, Hublot, and MB&F are all good examples of this in action. But now, combine that with the improvements we're seeing in the uses of the mainspring torque, we are entering a new era where true creative freedom is possible. In other words, apart from cost constraints, they can now create virtually any watch they can think of. As I said, Ressence is a great example – before, it was impossible to move such a heavy dial with magnets; now it's possible.

You said we're entering a new era of creativity. What creative opportunities will these changes present, do you think?

From a design and aesthetic perspective, we'll see even more refined and three-dimensional cases. With new machinery, creators will be able to produce different cases compared to before, and I think three-dimensional cases will become increasingly popular. The pebble-shaped case from Ressence is a good example of this. And then on the watchmaking front, I think we'll see larger mechanisms. That's the future of the watch industry.

When it comes to the independent brands that have experienced such growth in popularity over the past few years, do you see them becoming much bigger in the future?

What's interesting for me is that some watchmakers, like Ressence, MB&F, Urwerk, and others, prefer to stay smaller to keep their creativity. For them, that's the most important point, not their size. Perhaps they could produce more watches, but they're trying to keep their smaller size, to protect their purity and creativity.

How does all this make you feel, as a watch journalist who has been following the industry so closely for the past two decades?

The innovation we're seeing from avant-garde brands like Ressence is likely to trickle down across the industry. In other words, creativity will be seen across all price ranges. So for me, it's very important that brands like Ressence keep their creativity and continue using new materials and trying new things, because it provokes other watchmakers. Thanks to new technologies and the younger generation of talented, visionary watchmakers, innovation is accelerating. And in watchmaking, innovation is almost synonymous with creativity.

What do you think buyers and collectors will be looking for in the future? Do you think they're going to continue demanding smaller, more creative brands, like you've been talking about?

Definitely, I'm convinced that demand for small watchmakers and more ambitious watchmakers will be huge. But I also think the next ten years will be hard for certain smaller brands, because the market is so matured that collectors are really looking for a good all-round package. Maybe ten years ago, if a watch had one big attractive aspect, many collectors would have bought it. But today, you need to have everything – unique design and an interesting mechanism. Those watchmakers who create poor-quality watches with one big interesting mechanism will lose their status, but those with a good product and a good all-round package, their future will be brighter.

In terms of design and style, many watch experts say that we're in a more subtle and more classical era now. Big flashy watches that are overly showy are out of favour. Is that how you see things?

I agree with you. We're in an era of sophisticated, subtle taste. The tendency has become more classical, but it still needs to have a modern touch – it can't just be a rehash of watches from thirty years ago. And it doesn't have to be conservative. Now is the time of modern classical watches. I think Ressence is a good example of this. With Ressence, the way of showing the time is entirely different from conventional watches, but the concept is also quite classical, very sophisticated and it can be worn every day.

Do you think this modern classical era in terms of design and style is going to stay with us for the next few years? Or is it something you can see disappearing soon?

No, it's not a trend. It will be a period for the industry.

We've touched on technology a bit already – you've spoken about machining techniques and advancements in watch mechanisms – but how else might technology play a role in the future of the industry?

Thanks to new machinery and new ways of controlling the torque from the mainspring, we're now entering a new era for mechanical watches. You have Ressence with its magnetic floating time-indication system, which is so impressive; lighter silicon escapements will improve the frequency of mechanical movements and give a longer power reserve; and then new lubricants for the movement will improve the performance of mechanical watches. These innovations will change mechanical watches and open up new creative possibilities. I'm convinced that the future of mechanical watches will be brighter because of these new technologies.

"We're in an era of sophisticated, subtle taste. The tendency has become more classical, but it still needs to have a modern touch – it can't just be a rehash of watches from thirty years ago."

Staying with technology, so many industries are currently obsessed with AI. Can you see the watch industry being affected by AI in any way?

I don't think so. I know that Casio, the maker of the G-Shock watch, recently created a unique piece – with a gold case and gold bracelet – with the help of AI, but later chose to downplay that aspect in their messaging. They realised that AI itself doesn't hold much value in the eyes of the consumer. Yes, AI will become popular in the watch industry and will be used to improve the quality level of the case, the movement, the dial. But I think that creativity is not done by AI, but by human beings, and I'm convinced that human creativity is much more important, more precious, and also a more interesting sales point for customers.

Finally, more generally speaking, what creative or technological opportunities are you particularly excited about right now?

Personally, I'm fascinated by tribology, the science of friction and lubrication. Abraham-Louis Breguet once said that with perfect oil, he could build the perfect watch. I believe his inventions, like the natural escapement and tourbillon, were attempts to solve lubrication challenges. Today, we're seeing real progress with silicon components and new types of lubricants. With less resistance, it will be possible to move larger mechanisms with greater precision. These innovations reduce friction and open up new potential for mechanical watches.

John Jay

Jay is one of global branding's most respected cultural voices. From developing some of Nike's most impactful campaigns to shaping Uniqlo's global storytelling, he shows how design and commerce coexist without compromise. With a creative career defined by purpose, his perspective is essential to understanding how physical brands can continue to remain relevant in an increasingly digital future.

PRESIDENT OF GLOBAL CREATIVE AT FAST RETAILING

As President of Global Creative of Fast Retailing – the parent company of Uniqlo – John Jay helps define the mega-brand's timeless values, such as quality, authenticity, and human connection. In an era when marketing often means churning out bite-sized forms of 'content', Jay champions high-quality storytelling imbued with a deeper cultural meaning. A legend in the global advertising and design industry, for Jay, quality is nothing less than a moral imperative. At Uniqlo, he has made LifeWear – the brand's ethos of designing clothing that improves everyday life – a guiding principle, framing the company's commitment to well-crafted, long-lasting apparel. In doing so, he's proved that quality can also be accessible. As he puts it, his mission is "to create the highest quality of experiences for the greatest number of people on Earth" – a lofty goal that aligns with Uniqlo's democratic vision.

This values-driven philosophy has defined Jay's career for decades. Early in his career at Nike's agency Wieden+Kennedy, he preached cultural immersion over clever gimmicks – a mindset he carries into everything he does at Uniqlo. He listens first and never underestimates his audience. By honouring the audience's intelligence and identity, Jay turns customer communication into an act of empathy and cultural exchange.

Even as technology transforms the creative landscape, Jay remains steadfast that the future of creativity is fundamentally human. He greets developments like artificial intelligence with cautious optimism – seeing their potential to aid creativity but not to replace human intuition and imagination. In his view, humans remain the parents of technology, responsible for imparting it with standards and ethics. From championing global cultural storytelling to mentoring the next generation, John Jay exemplifies creative leadership that is both future-forward and deeply rooted in core values.

Professionally speaking, how do you define your guiding principles?

When I first met Yanai-san (Tadashi Yanai is a Japanese billionaire businessman and the founder and president of Fast Retailing, which owns Uniqlo), he asked for my advice and I said, "Always respect the intelligence of your consumer." Many marketing and advertising people think they're so clever. But people in my profession should never think of themselves as smarter than the audience they're speaking to.

What creative/ technological opportunities does the future hold? What are you particularly excited about?

It's a huge question. We are still, for at least a short time, the parents of AI. We are still the guiding force of AI. How we teach it, the process, the learning that we give it – if quality is embedded into our teaching and learning, it's like raising children.

When thinking about this, we must be conscious that quality is important. This goes for both AI and the next generations of humans. In this severe search for 'optimisation', the fancy word for 'profitability at all costs', we teach the next generation the wrong things. Right now, we are teaching the next generation to lower the bar of expectations.

How do you overcome that challenge in your line of work, given that you're dealing with a global consumer product, mega efficiencies, and many young people coming into your workforce?

The company's number one uncompromisable idea – and we're not always perfect – is quality. We will never compromise on the quality of the clothing, yet we're trying to make it affordable and accessible to the greatest number of people.

The easiest way to describe my job today is to create the highest-quality experiences for the largest number of people possible. Are our stores perfect? Is our service perfect? These are questions we need to address every day. Indeed, the marketing communications aren't yet at the level that I wish they could be. However, there is one subject that we do not ever compromise on: the quality of the clothing while making it accessible. That's that incredible balance that comes from our DNA.

You were encouraged earlier in your career to travel and experience culture, which gave you a broad view of how to speak to the world through your work. How does that fit into your guiding principles?

I started my career in journalism, but the real area where I grew was working with Bloomingdale's at its height. When I say that to people today, they have no idea what that era was or what American retailing was like at that time.

The first project I worked on was arguably the greatest retail promotion in the history of American retail – China: The Dawn of a New Era in 1979–80. Kissinger and Nixon had only opened the country up in 1972–73. This was the first major marketing project coming out of China at that time. I was in a country of over a billion people without automobiles, retail stores, or fashion, just uniforms. I was trying to figure out how to tell this story as China was emerging into the world.

Interestingly, many years later, Dan Wieden said at a management meeting in Rio, "Let's test our mission statement." We bounced around ideas. I was taking notes, and suddenly, Dan said, "I got it!" He rushed to the blackboard and wrote: "Be the eye of the cultural storm."

Long before I heard that, I was in that eye. Bloomingdale's took me all over the world. I worked with top designers and the Ministry of Education, the Ministry of Trade, and the Ministry of Culture in Paris, London, and China. *The New Yorker* had a famous tagline about us, 'the only retail store with its own foreign policy', because we featured all major countries. I was immersed in flying to every culture, getting deep into each one.

Marvin Traub, the genius and long-serving CEO and President of Bloomingdale's, threw me into the deep end, and we flew worldwide with him. My first trip to Japan was with Mr and Mrs Traub. I was lucky to be in the midst of that amazing era.

I was there for twelve years, then went to Wieden+Kennedy. I arrived on Monday without visiting Portland, seeing the agency, or interviewing there. I just knew that's where I needed to be to make the best work of my life. Phil Knight, Nike's founder, called on Thursday and said to Dan Wieden, "I believe our brand is suffering in New York. We're losing relevance on the streets of New York. What can we do about it?" Dan said, "My friend John just arrived from New York. Let me talk to him."

The result was an idea I created called City Attack. For marketers, it meant to go to a city, shut up, show respect, don't be so clever, and think you can 'market' your way out of a problem. The idea was to get deep into the fabric of the city and culture, meet influential people, meet the people on the streets, listen to them, and then come up with ideas to resolve the problem. That philosophy of City Attack is now one of the foundations of Nike marketing as they go around the world. Go deep into the culture, show your respect, then make some work. That part, in terms of storytelling and getting deep into culture, is my best contribution to the brand, and I'm proud to say it's still one of the foundations of their global marketing today.

What do you see in the cultural sphere that will remain important in fifteen years' time?

We need to be physical with how we interact with ourselves and the world, which will always be relevant. That is why reading and book clubs are the hottest things in America right now, and paperbacks have become *the* fashion accessory. Young people are reading together. I built the Global Creative Lab for Fast Retailing – and, in the case of Uniqlo, opened offices in Tokyo and Shanghai, as well as New York City – to create centres of excellence for people to gather. Everyone has to come to work to work in my office. We meet; we get together. I just invested in magnetic boards on all the walls to return to the tradition of putting stuff on the wall, taking it down, placing a headline on top of that picture, changing it, and arguing about ideas in person.

And is this the future of work for many industries, not just creative ones?

I hope so. Right now, Gen Z people in America are taking lessons on how to speak on the phone because they're scared to death. 80% of them say they don't answer any phone calls. They're afraid – not just of talking in person – they're scared to pick up a phone and talk with a human being in real time. The future is human. ==Humanity is back to getting together as a community.== Community building is so important in America right now, especially with young people.

==**"The future is human."**==

What's 'the next big thing' in your industry/field, and how might it impact our lives? How does it make you feel?

You can't escape AI. That is the current thing, and it will be the future thing. Certain people will say that graphic designers or editors will be, within five years, no longer necessary. I don't believe that because humanity, intuition, and imagination are fed into us from many sources. It's not just reading off of a screen. ==I have great faith in humanity, but we have to be careful. We have to put the proper mechanisms in place and help young people to appreciate things that are real in life.==

You can't escape technology, and now it's speeding along at a faster rate, with the technological war between the East and the West, with China in particular. That means I can learn a subject more quickly and more deeply through that technology. I can be better informed, at least from an informational standpoint, than ever before. I can do a mood board all over the world and have some help in doing that. It helps me to get more information, but it's still up to me to choose what information to put in the hierarchy. What's one, two, and three? I have to use my imagination and my heart.

Some people have an excellent head, but it's not connected to the heart, and that's not connected to the gut. There's a reason why people still say, 'trust your gut'.

Will we be able to develop gut instincts faster? A gut instinct can come from taste, so will we see the acceleration of developing taste?

For centuries, we've debated 'what is taste?' But taste is an accumulation of experiences. Can your taste develop from looking at a flat-screen? I don't think so. You can look at food from Morocco on a screen online, but until you sit down and have dinner in Morocco, pull the meat with your hands, and sit next to people who don't look like you, you'll never know what the food you're looking at means. Travelling is the greatest way to bring you back to earth because it immediately teaches you how little you know. It's the great equaliser.

For you, what does quality time mean?

To be honest with you, I don't get enough of it. My curiosity can get the best of me. I'm always interested in lots of new projects. I'm in an excellent position to have interesting people cross my path. I love that part of my life.

==Family is primary, the most important.== If I can be more personal, the most significant change in my life in the last two years was when I lost my young son. He was a filmmaker who gave up filmmaking to become a beautiful community builder, bringing young, emerging artists from Japan to the Pacific Northwest. I'm working a lot in my off-time on his legacy, growing the concept. It's called End of Summer and it happens every August.

Moving back to Uniqlo, it's a very physical brand with many real-life stores. But how important is augmented reality, and where is this field heading?

We're all exploring that. Retailers have been studying it for decades, for years and years. We're getting better and better. We're not there yet, but the future will include that.

Think about the 'magic mirror' – how many years have we been trying to develop that? It's a concept where you walk into the dressing room and don't have to try the clothes on. You can try on fifteen outfits in different colours virtually. The industry has been talking about that ad nauseam. Technology is getting closer to enabling this, but we must be smart about it. If the consumer uses it to better understand and make choices about our clothing, we cannot shy away from it. ==But coming into a real store and feeling the ambience and the people who touch you and treat you is still important. This type of retail is our home.==

How do you imagine this high street of the future?

At the end of the day, "Do you have what I want in my size and colour?" This is still the rule in brick-and-mortar retail. So, too, is asking, "Are we making clothes relevant to your life?" This is why LifeWear is our central concept. Everything we do, not only the clothes but also our course of action and how we act as a citizen of the world, is under the umbrella of LifeWear.

The concept of LifeWear is so essential, and it's so typically Japanese. It's very simple. It's deceivingly simple – LifeWear, meaning clothing for your life, relevant for all facets of your life, meaning that we will never be a fast fashion company because we will never think of disposable clothing as something we make. We want our cashmere to last you for ten years. We hope that the Oxford shirt you buy lasts you for five years. That's why it's called LifeWear. It's a manifestation to show our deep respect for everyone.

LifeWear is extraordinarily important. I'm so deeply immersed in it right now that it's almost hard to talk about it. How do we elevate the standard of living for everyone? How do we make high-quality clothing accessible for everyone? How can we challenge the norms of what is quality? LifeWear is helping us redefine the very concept of value. Our clothes keep getting better and better, but the prices remain fairly stable and affordable. Ultimately, that is a sign of respect.

"I hope the next big things are kindness, empathy, fairness, respect, and maybe even, God forbid, the truth."

Are you positive that quality will always win out in the future?

At Uniqlo, we discuss this openly. Whether or not that spreads throughout the entire company, we'll see. But you cannot take anything for granted right now. I have this thing that I talk about, 'algorithms of mediocrity'. The algorithms are driving mediocrity in our lives, and we're becoming more accepting of it.

Do we need to work hard to programme our way out of this?

Yes! When you asked the question earlier about the next big thing, of course, you can't escape AI, but I'd like to think of the answer in a different way. When we asked Roger Federer what makes life better – because that was my campaign a few months ago as part of LifeWear Day – he said kindness. When we asked Christophe Lemaire about it, he said it was poetry. These are the answers we need to answer your question. So, I hope the next big things are kindness, empathy, fairness, respect, and maybe even, God forbid, the truth.

Finally, is there anything you'd like to add?

These conversations are important for all the reasons I said, and I'm proud to say I work for a company that represents these values. It's not bullshit. I'm from creativity and design. I can smell bullshit a mile away.

Are we flawed? Are we human? Are we imperfect? Of course we are. We use a thing in Japan called the *shinzenbi* philosophy as a driving force of our company that we never talk about openly. It's truth, goodness, and beauty – that's the driving force of our company. Often in boardrooms, we say, "Don't forget *shinzenbi*." Go to Wall Street, a public company in America, walk into a boardroom, and say, "Ladies and gentlemen, I'd like to talk to you today about truth, honesty, values, and beauty." You'd be booted out into the hallway. For us, this philosophy is the water we drink.

"Go to Wall Street, a public company in America, walk into a boardroom, and say, 'Ladies and gentlemen, I'd like to talk to you today about truth, honesty, values, and beauty.' You'd be booted out into the hallway. For us, this philosophy is the water we drink."

John Jay

Tiina Karjalainen Kierysch

HEAD OF DESIGN AT BANG & OLUFSEN

Karjalainen Kierysch shapes how we live with technology as Head of Design at Bang & Olufsen. Blending Scandinavian minimalism and emotional resonance, she crafts audio experiences as mindful rituals rather than mere routines. Her forward-thinking approach embraces digital craftsmanship and AI-enhanced personalisation, pushing high-end design beyond aesthetics to create meaningful, lasting interactions between humans and technology.

Tiina Karjalainen Kierysch, a Finnish-Swedish designer, doesn't approach her craft as a static discipline – she sees it as a fluid tool for shaping how we live with technology. After early roles designing mobile phones at Sony Ericsson, and later developing smart wearables at Sony, she joined Bang & Olufsen a decade ago. Since then, she has steadily expanded her role. She started working with brand partnership designs and moved from there to leading the Colour, Material and Finish team (CMF). A couple of years later she expanded to leading Industrial Design and today she is heading up design overall – helping guide the future of one of the most respected names in high-end audio.

Founded in 1925 in Struer, Denmark, Bang & Olufsen has long stood apart from the mainstream of the consumer electronics industry. Known for its sculptural, often radical hardware and uncompromising approach to audio quality, the company has consistently merged innovative engineering with cultural expression. At Bang & Olufsen, Karjalainen Kierisch champions thoughtfulness and care during concept creation, fostering a more reflective and even ritualistic relationship with technology. The goal isn't just convenience – it's presence, memory, atmosphere. "Instead of seeing it as a routine where you just put a device on, it could become a ritual", she says.

With an eye on the brand's prestigious past, Karjalainen Kierysch brings a future-minded lens to everything she and her design team work on. That includes rethinking how craftsmanship extends into the digital realm, where behaviours, interaction and sensorial experiences are just as vital as tactility. She talks about 'crafting the digital experience' with the same care as machining aluminium or tuning acoustics. That care extends to longevity as well. Whether through modular construction, software upgradeability, or reviving legacy products through new connectivity, she sees keeping things in use – not simply making replacements – as a powerful design statement.

Bang & Olufsen's long-standing resistance to convention makes it fertile ground for this type of thinking. Karjalainen Kierysch sees its design culture not just as Nordic, but future-facing – unafraid to ask what a speaker, a system, or even a brand should become. Under her direction, design is not decoration, it's a framework for navigating complexity. Technology is getting smarter – but so, she suggests, should our relationship with it.

Bang & Olufsen still prioritises industrial design, despite creating very high-tech pieces of hardware. So, what is the experience like leading design there?

Yes, Bang & Olufsen places a great emphasis on industrial design and will continue to do so. The way we differ is that we have consistently approached our industry in a unique way compared to traditional consumer electronics brands. We have a philosophy and a mindset that dates back to our founders, who opened the company in 1925. They had a vision and a mission, and they summarised it as a never-failing will to create only the best and never cease to find improvements. So, there's always this mindset: how can we continually improve, but at the same time, how can we approach things differently? So when you ask what that's like, that's one of the most fascinating parts about being involved with Bang & Olufsen. It's part of our DNA to challenge the industry and challenge the status quo. And sometimes we even go so far as to think about how we can challenge a category of products. For instance, in the 1990s, when CD players were black boxes, the Beogram 9000 was developed with its mechanism on display; it was an entirely new way of presenting the category.

Is there still room to elevate and innovate in these categories?

Yes. Again, we view things differently, not only in terms of industrial design, but also in how we interact with our products. We spend a considerable amount of time discussing this with the team every week. And what we have landed on is that we would rather see our products move to a space where, instead of seeing it as a routine where you just put a device on, it could become a ritual. Imagine having a very special tea that you would like to enjoy, with a particular ritual surrounding the act of using your favourite teapot, your beloved teacup, and all the accompanying items. A similar type of ritual can also occur when interacting with audio devices. ==If we consider how quickly everything has to go today, and you do everything through your device, there's also something soothing and calming about letting things take their time.== We would love to expand on this idea further.

And how do you develop that?

As a company, we often discuss sound design and craft, and the craft aspect is traditionally thought of in terms of physical manufacturing. We also draw inspiration from handcraft techniques that we incorporate. We are increasingly thinking about how to craft the digital experience. I see the craft space and craftsmanship transitioning into a phygital realm (a term for the hybridisation of physical and digital), encompassing more immersive sensory experience as well, which is super exciting territory.

So you see, for the future, a more meaningful and deeper way of interacting with technology?

Yes. And there will be brands thinking about it differently. Here, we aim to create experiences that surpass the ordinary or mundane, and the experiential aspect plays a huge part in this. At Bang & Olufsen, we internally refer to our products as having different types of magic. And what we mean by that is that there's something delightful and surprising about them and the experiences we have through them. And of course, this magic that we think about, how can we deepen that magic for the future, with the technologies of the future as well?

Nordic nations are renowned for their considered design, which encourages people to slow down and appreciate elements such as tactility and quality. Do you think people will value products that are more thoughtfully designed in the future?

I think they will. And there's some counterpart needed towards this fast-paced world that we're living in, so to stay grounded we will need means and ways to balance that. And here, the calmness that Scandinavian design can bring is a great support.

"We are increasingly thinking about how to craft the digital experience. I see the craft space and craftsmanship transitioning into a phygital realm, encompassing even more immersive sensory experiences."

Professionally speaking, how do you define your guiding principles?

When it comes to design, I don't have aesthetic guiding principles or anything like that. I have, instead, guiding principles in terms of mindset – how to approach design. And the first piece that's foundational to the way I work, and how my teams work, is that it's essential for the creative contributions coming from the team to be well-considered and that the designs we create evoke emotions.

It's a lot about curiosity. Curiosity is a key enabler for designers to delve deeper into imaginative worlds and explore the research they are conducting, as well as to be curious about the world around them. Curiosity is foundational and essential when working with design. Additionally, the other part of that is that unique ideas often come from intense curiosity. They come when you are really open and just daring to question things. That's when you start entering new territory as well. Another principle that we, as a team at Bang & Olufsen, also hold is to make sure that our customers can feel the care we put into our products. If we show respect to the process, the customers, and the manufacturing methods, that care will, in the end, be felt in the product. It could be an intangible thing. Perhaps you can't fully understand what it is, but as a whole, you will think that somebody has truly put their heart and soul into this.

Finally, on this list of personal motivation drivers, circularity is a big one. As designers, we should all feel the responsibility of not just adding products to the world, but adding meaningful products to the world, and then really trying to do everything that we can to keep them as circular as possible, and influence through pushing the boundaries of what can be done so that we can inspire others to join.

*What's 'the next big thing' in your industry or field?
What technologies are you particularly excited about?*

So listening to sound is, of course, a very emotional experience, and every technology that can help us get even further immersed in sound or music will be interesting. There are fantastic developments taking place in the field of spatial sound. That is interesting for the future – how we can delve even deeper into our musical experiences with spatial sound. In the future, we will be able to adapt sound much more closely to where the customers are, how they're feeling and how they're doing. So, we expect future technologies may help the industry form experiences within that context, whereas perhaps we have previously considered use cases in a more traditional way.

Additionally, sound will become an even bigger part of the product interaction, as well as the way brands are branding themselves sonically. How do you sound as a brand, as a car brand, or how do you sound as a smart wearable?

Is that something you're having a lot of conversations about now, sound branding?

There's so much to a product's character, encompassing its appearance, touch, feel, colours, and even the interaction – not just the tactile interaction, but also the way sound interacts with you – those will all form a stronger identity.

And then, going back to what you were saying before, about the engineering of the sound quality and soundscapes. Where is it at now, and where can it go?

==Combining sound, spatial sound, and AI can take us to an even more immersive, interactive, and emotionally engaging space.== We think a lot about orchestrating experiences at Bang & Olufsen, and that's particularly interesting for us in terms of what we could do with sound, spatial audio, and AI in this context. We've done some work on augmented sound, which enables us to create different environments. We've collaborated with some of our automotive partners on this, so that when you sit in a vehicle, it can sound like you're in a church. That will also significantly enhance emotional experiences, making you feel as though you are somewhere else.

Also, the other tangible thing I'm thinking about – and now, without talking about the technologies themselves – is what can be done with them. In our everyday lives, there are many moments when we are in flux and things are not working as expected. We will be in more of a flow with sounds that can support what we're doing in the moment. Perhaps, when we're discussing – like we are today – on a video call, you and I will almost feel like we're in the same room. What if the sound made it feel like we're sitting in my living room or yours? Alternatively, it could be that sound can be more supportive of you during the activities you're doing – maybe you want to focus or block out everything else. So there's a lot to this – sound will, in the future, support us much more with the things that we want to be doing in the moment.

> "Sound will, in the future, support us much more with the things that we want to be doing in the moment."

Could you discuss your approach to sustainability as a company and as a designer, and where do you see this heading in the future?

Longevity is, of course, vital for us. We would want our customers to pass the product on to the next generation. It's a bit of a Scandinavian or Danish thing that, for instance, with Bang & Olufsen speakers or TVs, you might first have them in your home. Then, your child moves away from home, and you acquire something else. The child inherits it, and then they get a new home. Eventually, the technology can move to the summer house. Since we put so much love and care into our products, and they continue to function exceptionally well after all these years, why would you consider getting rid of them? There's no need.

Another thing is that we want to support the longevity strategy in different ways. And the first is that we can repair and exchange parts in case something no longer functions. And to be able to do that, we have been working in a very modular way with our products. Another thing is the software's upgradeability. We want to ensure that the product can last a long time through the platforms we have and then be upgraded. We work with the Cradle to Cradle eco-label certification, a highly ambitious eco-certification that helps us assess our circularity performance. And now we have eight products that are Cradle to Cradle certified. This means that we can offer Cradle to Cradle certified products for all sound use cases, whether it's for on-the-go speakers or wearables, or in your home with vision and sound.

Another branch of the longevity piece are our recreated classics products. We can now connect old products to new technology and also to our app, which is mind-blowing for me as a designer. We're working with our future portfolio, but we're also working with our past portfolio. Old products can come back to life through connectivity and modern technology.

Daniel Libeskind

FOUNDER OF STUDIO LIBESKIND

Libeskind designs architecture charged with memory and meaning. His landmark projects – including the Jewish Museum Berlin and the World Trade Center Master Plan – embody powerful narratives of loss, recovery, and resilience. At a time when urban development risks generic outcomes, Libeskind remains a vital advocate for culturally sensitive, historically informed built environments.

World-renowned architect Daniel Libeskind made his name with buildings that represented and memorialised tragic histories, such as the Jewish Museum in Berlin and the Military History Museum in Dresden. In 2003, he began what is arguably his most high-profile project to date when he won a global competition to design the overarching World Trade Center Master Plan, the redevelopment of the site in New York where the Twin Towers once stood.

The son of Jewish Holocaust survivors, Libeskind has never shied away from such poignant and emotionally charged projects, believing architecture to be an art form that has to connect with people on an emotional level. As he puts it, "Our life is not made up only of logic, calculation, and transaction. It's primarily lived in an emotional way, in a spiritual way. Architecture, in the same way, has to touch on the emotions."

This is not to say that architecture necessarily needs to make people feel good, according to Libeskind. Indeed, what has become recognised as his trademark style – characterised by sharp angles and fragmented forms – is sometimes specifically designed to make those in its midst feel discomfort. This is perhaps clearest in his design for Berlin's Jewish Museum, which opened to the public in 2001 and makes visitors experience the full gamut of human emotion. The project initially divided opinion within the architecture community for its unconventional approach, but has widely come to be seen as a masterpiece of modern architecture.

Aside from these projects, Studio Libeskind has also designed a wide range of buildings all over the globe, from a mixed-use tower in Manila to a hotel and residential building in Dubai. More recently, Libeskind was behind the design of the Einstein House, a building currently under construction in Jerusalem that will house the legacy and work of Nobel laureate Albert Einstein. The striking design features a twisted cube that is angled skywards, creating a complex geometry inspired by Einstein's own mathematical research. The project reaffirms what many already know – that Daniel Libeskind is one of the most versatile, original, and forward-looking architects working today.

In this wide-ranging interview, Libeskind discusses how technology is impacting the field of architecture, why memory and history are the key to building the future, and how our cities are really reflections of our society and culture.

Professionally speaking, how do you define your guiding principles?

What is true, what is beautiful, and what is good. Those are the great, ancient values that I subscribe to. Truth in architecture means authenticity, an authentic response, not a stylised one or a simulation, but really delving into the truth of the project and its place in the world. Good in architecture means sustainable, something which will last forever, not just an exercise in commodities. And what is beautiful is beautiful. You can't define beauty. It just is or it isn't.

What's 'the next big thing' in architecture, and how might it impact our lives?

There will be, of course, a technological aspect – new discoveries in the physics of materials and the technology of construction to make it more efficient, because building is a very ancient exercise and it hasn't changed that much in thousands of years. There will be great leaps forwards in how buildings are built. And, of course, artificial intelligence, which will make design completely robotic, and also robots will be used in construction. The big challenge will be: where is the human value of all of this development? How will architecture be relevant to human beings using these artificial means? The art of architecture will be in danger. And architecture as just a commercial product that is manufactured in factories will be commonplace. Will there be an art of architecture, or will it all be just a simulated field of building?

"There will be great leaps forwards in how buildings are built ... The big challenge will be: where is the human value of all of this development? ... Will there be an art of architecture, or will it all be just a simulated field of building?"

We tend to think about AI predominantly in the world of software these days, but you're saying even architecture, which is such a physical practice, will be affected by it?

> It is already. Many offices don't really have human beings designing anything, it's all designed by AI. And I think we will see this artificial, simulated product, which looks nice at first, but when you look at it closely, it lacks all artistic meaning, because it's just a fake collage of already pre-existing forms and ideas.

As someone who has given his whole career to making, as you said, beautiful buildings, how does that make you feel?

> I think it will make architecture even more desirable, because it will separate the technological production from the artistic production of architecture. It will be desirable to find architects who can still work on a human level and with a certain spirit. It's similar to buying a mass-produced, off-the-rack suit and buying a custom-made suit tailored to your proportions, and to your liking.

Another technology that the architectural world has been quick to embrace is virtual reality for visualising designs. What impact might that have?

No doubt about it, that immersive idea of communicating design is already here. People want to have that feeling of what the building will be like, so using this new technology will become the formula. But there is also a problem here, because whatever you can get through a virtual experience of architecture, it will not be the same as the architectural experience itself. Architecture depends on your body, on your gravity, and on your whole emotional response. It's one of the few fields that cannot really thrive on virtual technology. We can do all the acrobatics with technology, but we are alive, we have bodies that are more than just our brains. That's the enigma of the human condition. Maybe at some point we will just be brains, and we will not move around, like in science fiction. But I would not call that life.

When you look ahead, what creative opportunities will this future present for architects?

The creative part is to understand the history of the city, not treating the city like a *tabula rasa* for utopian dreams, but really using the history of the city to bring out its best. That means adaptive reuse of buildings, and also, of course, finding new ways of bringing something completely new to the city through structures that are unprecedented.

> "Without memory, the city becomes a demented operation … Memory, to me, is the ground of architecture … It's the memory that keeps the shape of the city – not the bricks, not the steel."

So much of your work has been about memory, about understanding history and bringing it to life in the form of architecture. Do you worry that sometimes modern architecture is too 'utopian', that it has lost its foundation within memory?

Definitely. Without memory, the city becomes a demented operation. We are like people with Alzheimer's who don't recognise where they are. Memory, to me, is the ground of architecture. If architecture and the city do not really lock themselves to the foundations of memory, they'll be producing things that won't last a long time, because it's the memory that keeps the shape of the city – not the bricks, not the steel.

How does this connect to your thoughts around sustainability? You've spoken in the past about how sustainability is the way in which people relate to a building over a long period of time.

That's right. What is sustainable is the memory. That's why we keep things, why we love things, and take care of them, because we relate to them in the depths of time. Without that relationship, things are just objects in space that don't have particular validity for us as human beings. ==For something to be built to last, it has to be really well conceived. It's not just a trick of the latest technology.== It has to really last and outlast all the desires that we have today and provide a space for future desires. That's why we love traditional buildings, why we love old temples, even ruins, because we see that they survived their own era, because they had a cultural and spiritual content. Without this content, architecture in the city will become really prone to the plague of fashion.

Talk us through the World Trade Center Master Plan and how you approached that challenge, with all of these ideas of memory and sustainability in mind.

That was my first radical departure from the rest of my colleagues, which was to decide not to build where people perished. The seven competing architects all built exactly where the buildings once stood. But I felt it wasn't right. We have to acknowledge that this is no longer just a secular space that we can do whatever we want with; there is a spiritual aspect, because people perished in their thousands. We cannot build here. So I left the centre of the site as a memory, as a memorial, with accessibility to the deep foundations, to the bedrock of New York. That is really the centre of my project – the sense that you have to encounter that memory to understand the buildings, which are then spaced around it. And at the same time, we created a vibrant neighbourhood with state-of-the-art buildings, which are shaped around the space in a symbolic way, to create an ensemble that is both looking back towards the event but also looking towards the future of New York.

That project perfectly reflects your humanistic approach to design. Looking ahead, what impact might the architecture of the future have on people's lives?

We have to bring the political arena in here, because we need equality and democracy in the city. The danger is that we have a segregated city, one for the rich and one for the poor, which is, of course, already a growing danger. It will be a huge challenge to create an integrated whole, where people of all sorts can thrive. And I think it's a challenge for democracy. How can we give the benefits of the city not just to the few, but to its entire working public? I really think this is the most important thing for the future: how to create new typologies with dignity and beauty for people in cities. Not just the buildings that we often venerate, which are for the very wealthy, but buildings for regular people.

Lastly, what still keeps you excited and energised about the field of architecture?

What gets me energised about the future of architecture is that it is, I would almost say, the solitary art among all the great arts that creates a place for people in a real way, and that will never go away. There will always be a desire, from ancient times to the distant future, to have a meaningful place, to have meaning in space. And I think that meaning is, of course, also forever changing. Architecture holds up a mirror to who we are. When you look at a city, it mirrors the time we live in. When we look at old cities, they mirror the cultures of those times. Whatever technological changes, whatever futuristic changes, whatever new things come into it, architecture will always be hinged on the human soul. It will never be detached from it, because it's who we are, how we walk, how we get up in the morning, how we look out onto the street, what we feel about other people. Everything is architecture, that's why it's such an exciting field.

Virgilio Martínez

CHEF AND RESTAURATEUR

Martínez is one of the world's most innovative chefs. At his restaurant Central, he explores Peru's ecosystems by crafting menus based on their altitudes and native ingredients. His approach uniquely blends indigenous agricultural knowledge, ecology, and gastronomy, offering a compelling blueprint for a more thoughtful and sustainable future of food.

Virgilio Martínez's rise in recent years to the pinnacle of global gastronomy is the culmination of a lifelong mission to master the craft of cooking. Born in Lima, Peru, Martínez originally decided to become a chef because he wanted to travel the world, and so he went to study at the famous cookery school Le Cordon Bleu in both Ottawa and London. After graduating in 1998, he spent the next decade working in some of the best fine dining restaurants on the planet, from Lutèce in New York to Can Fabes in Spain.

However, it was only when he returned to his native Peru that Martínez had his lightbulb moment. He came back to a country that was undergoing an exciting gastronomic boom, but none of the new restaurants were, to his mind, doing enough to showcase the country's extraordinary biodiversity, indigenous ingredients, traditional cooking techniques, and remarkable natural habitats. So, in 2009, Martínez opened his own restaurant in Lima, called Central, which sought to celebrate these wonders of Peru.

Over the following decade, Central's reputation grew steadily, until it was recognised in 2023 as the best restaurant on the planet at the World's 50 Best Restaurants Awards – becoming the first restaurant outside Europe and the USA to achieve this honour. The menu takes guests through a range of Peruvian 'ecosystems', as it describes them, arranged according to altitude, diving down to below sea level for one course and then climbing the peaks of the Andes for the next. Each dish uses ingredients from its respective altitude in highly innovative and creative ways.

However, whilst Central has won the plaudits, MIL Centro is where Martínez feels his ethos around gastronomy is most tangible. Opened in 2018, the restaurant and research centre is situated around 3,500 metres above sea level in the Sacred Valley of Peru. The restaurant relies upon a symbiotic relationship with two local communities, which farm the land and harvest the ingredients for the kitchen. "There are three hundred families living and working with us", says Martínez. "It's not the way a restaurant normally works. It's coming from the communities."

Martínez's success to date has been achieved by pushing beyond the traditional limits of fine dining. Central's focus on meticulous research, on exploration and discovery – all in the service of bringing new, unique, and authentic experiences to its guests – struck a chord with diners searching for something new, driven by a meaningful purpose. Now, the chef and restaurateur is looking towards a new frontier in gastronomy, with his recently launched Immersions: full-day itineraries taking guests behind the scenes at Central and MIL. These experiences give diners a deeper insight, for instance, into how the restaurants work with indigenous communities to preserve traditional ingredients and cooking techniques.

As he tells us in this conversation, Martínez believes that these Immersions represent the future of high-end gastronomy. As he puts it, he has always focused on the 'exploration of new territories', and this is now what diners want more and more. "People want to explore new things," he says, "it's about a change, about experiencing something truly new."

You've had this incredible career that has taken you all over the globe. Throughout that time working in gastronomy, what have been your guiding principles? What are the things right at the centre of your philosophy of cooking and hospitality?

Lately, I've been talking a lot about discipline – how to improve through discipline, through repetition, through good habits. As a result, you get a very neat and beautiful technique, you have a nice group of people, a nice environment in the kitchen, and then the restaurant becomes amazing. It's not exactly a law of attraction, but when you have all this, you tend to get nice guests who are coming for something special. In our case, we're always searching for new things, an exploration of new territories. And when we achieve that, I feel that our guests are coming for the same thing. They're coming to explore new things.

You spoke about discipline and it feels like that is very much about running a team, running a kitchen. In terms of food and cooking, what would you say are your guiding principles?

We never compromise on the importance of the origin of ingredients. We go to MIL in Cusco and we're surrounded by nature, by local communities, people, and farmers. We have a few research centres and we're always searching for the truth in gastronomy – it's very important to us to know the origin of our ingredients, to know what's behind that ingredient. There's always a farmer and not only one farmer, but a family. We're always looking to support the well-being of everyone, which is why we never compromise when it comes to food and money either. ==We try to get our creativity from nature, people, and good environments.== That has been working for us and it's also giving us an elevated purpose and the emotion to achieve new things.

For you, what's 'the next big thing' in the field of food, gastronomy, and cooking? Is there an innovation or a new wave that you see coming that's particularly exciting, perhaps?

Previously, it used to be whatever was the latest thing. You'd hear, "Korea is going to be the next destination, Japan will be next, Peru will be the next gastronomy destination." It has changed a lot nowadays because we are overstimulated with communication; it can feel like we are everywhere at the same time. If you want to feel like you're in Paris or Tokyo, you can check your screen. I know everybody talks about authenticity, but that has to go to the next level. Everything needs to have a purpose. I have been working a lot at MIL, my restaurant in Cusco, which is in a rural area. I've realised that I get more emotional. Guests start to get more emotional when they go to these faraway places, where they can see a restaurant has another narrative, coming from the roots of nature. That's the next level – yes, nature, but authentic nature. Over the past ten years, we've been doing interpretations of nature, but it's not natural.

Do you feel that there needs to be a lot more of a story behind the food? What you're talking about seems to be less about new techniques or new science in gastronomy and more about narrative, the storytelling behind the food. Is that becoming more important?

At Central, we say we're cooking ecosystems and cooking with people. So, of course, you need a narrative, but you need to understand that nobody will come to you just because you have a strong narrative. We need to provide context. That's why for the past year, we've been doing these things we call Immersions, where we take guests behind the scenes and show them the *why*. This kind of immersive experience will be the trend. You leave your phone, your WhatsApp, your Instagram, and you don't take any photos. You're just there and committed to understanding what's happening there. It's a lot of work for the restaurant, because we need to provide more context, more information, and the information has to be real. We already have too many storytellers now; we need to turn the story into something real.

"Guests start to get more emotional when they go to these faraway places, where they can see a restaurant has another narrative, coming from the roots of nature."

Virgilio Martínez

That word 'immersive' is interesting. Is that where you see the world of fine dining going in the coming years? And if so, what creative opportunities will that present?

If you ask me what haute cuisine or fine dining will look like, I think it will be fewer people in dining rooms, bigger spaces, more isolated, and more private, where people can see a lot in one experience. We're planning to do this even more; we're working on it right now. So, if you want, we'll be able to give you the Central experience in the Peruvian Amazonia for a group of three people, and you can have 50 people working for you. If you want to go with our team on an exploration trip to the Amazon or to the mountains, you can join them.

For example, if I go to China in two weeks, I might want to eat something from one region cooked by a local in their house. My dream might be to have the whole neighbourhood cooking for me. That experience will cost me a lot of money, because the whole neighbourhood is cooking just for me and I'm going to have access to one specific house in this rural area. It will be more immersive, and it will go beyond a restaurant. But for me, it will give me the best understanding of this ecosystem and how people are related to agriculture and food, and how people are enjoying life and struggling, and much more.

> "If you ask me what haute cuisine or fine dining will look like, I think it will be fewer people in dining rooms, bigger spaces, more isolated, and more private, where people can see a lot in one experience."

That would be quite a big redefinition of what 'luxury' means in the context of food, wouldn't it?

What used to be cool five years ago is now already quite repetitive. Fine dining used to be about caviar, champagne, truffles, Wagyu meat – these five or ten key ingredients that you have to use. But my little kid is obsessively watching this guy eating Wagyu beef in Japan. My son is nine years old and he knows more about beef than I do! So when he goes to a restaurant now and eats Wagyu beef, he isn't that impressed – it's not new for him. But this used to be a luxury.

Fine dining isn't about that kind of luxury anymore. We've got to give you something else and it has to be more elevated. If you go to a place, you need the context. Luxury will be going to MIL and having no idea what to expect. Because who doesn't like to be surprised? Nowadays it's very easy to have a good idea of what something will be like before you go. But what about if you went there and something totally new happened, you tasted unknown ingredients, had unknown experiences, and enjoyed this new era of gastronomy?

You spoke there about how we've all been exposed to Wagyu beef now – even your nine-year-old son knows a lot about it. Is that an impact of modern social media on the gastronomy world and, if so, what might the impact be in the future, for both diners and people like you who own hospitality businesses?

Well, we're overstimulated with news, with tragic things happening in the world, with climate change, and the feeling that everything is going in a bad direction. The same is happening in gastronomy in a way. We're overstimulated with news about gastronomy, with trends, new techniques, and 'food porn'. That could be really good, but it also scares me a bit how the level of news is impacting our brains and our habits. We need to be more aware and conscious about these things, and we need to educate ourselves towards better habits with food.

The challenge for restaurant owners will be how much information, how much technology, how many screens, and how many special effects people are consuming. Our competition will be what people are seeing on social media and the expectations they have. So, when we're giving them something, it has to be very real and very natural, and the guest needs to have the space and the time to process it all.

It's clear that a lot of what you're saying is about removing technology from our lives – leaving our phones at the door, so we can fully experience something. But is there a role for technology to play in the future of the restaurant business?

Yes, of course. It might sound like I don't want any technology, but for sure, technology will be key. We need to be on top of it because all the information is in the palm of your hand. We've got to explore new possibilities in this digital world. Say if you wanted to join my team to go exploring in the Amazon, or maybe me when I go to Cusco tomorrow, if you want to join these trips, you'll still use digital tools to get the information, the news, and whatever you need. So it goes hand in hand with all the ideas about nature that we've been discussing.

"I think if we're not getting inspired by the future, we're losing it. I need to wake up and have this sense that I have a purpose being here. I have to see myself as an innovator."

The future you've been talking about, how does it make you feel? It sounds like you're both optimistic and inspired, but also a bit cautious.

I think if we're not getting inspired by the future, we're losing it. I need to wake up and have this sense that I have a purpose being here. I have to see myself as an innovator. I'm not saying I'm Ferran Adrià (legendary innovative Spanish chef) or whatever, but in my location here, we're innovating. People are coming to Lima to have an experience, flying to Cusco to have an experience. I get inspiration from that. We're about to serve lunch today and we're going to have fifteen different nationalities here in the dining room. That means different languages, different cultures. Every single day I get to learn something – but not from social media or the internet, from the restaurant. I see this in a very positive way. It could be scary, for sure, but you've got to take the positive side. It's a privilege to pass information on and receive information back.

"We're overstimulated with news, with tragic things happening in the world, with climate change, and the feeling that everything is going in a bad direction. The same is happening in gastronomy in a way. We're overstimulated with news about gastronomy, with trends, new techniques, and 'food porn'."

Lastly, more generally speaking, what creative opportunities does the future hold? What are you particularly excited about?

I feel more comfortable when I feel like there is a purpose to high-end gastronomy and a purpose behind people spending lots of money on these things. At MIL, I can see that higher purpose very easily, because good energy comes to you when you visit. When I go to cook there, I feel like we're doing something that is harmonised with nature and with the people.

Garry Nolan

Stanford professor and biotech pioneer Garry Nolan creates breakthrough technologies for medicine, decoding how immune cells function and diseases develop. His fearless approach – spanning from advanced cancer diagnostics to investigations into extraterrestrial life – makes him uniquely positioned to guide conversations around the future intersections of science, technology, and our understanding of intelligence.

PROFESSOR AT
STANFORD UNIVERSITY

Stanford professor Garry Nolan has built a career on turning what we would imagine as science fiction into reality. An immunologist turned inventor, Nolan is known for developing biotech and diagnostic tools that have transformed medicine, and for fearlessly venturing into scientific frontiers others shy away from. Over three decades, he has spun cutting-edge research in pathology, genetics, and atomic-scale imaging into half a dozen start-ups, pioneering technologies such as advanced cell analysis and high-resolution instrumentation. At the same time, he's applied his systems-level thinking to the ultimate outlier question: *are we alone in the universe?* His world view is both optimistic and controversial – a blend of a future-focused vision and a refusal to accept conventional limits.

Nolan often talks about 'reverse-engineering the future', envisioning where technology is headed and working backwards to build it today. In the lab, this means harnessing anomalies as clues to advance science. In the 1990s, that mindset led him to co-create a breakthrough gene-delivery system; more recently it drove him to analyse enigmatic materials purported to be of unknown origin. For him, curiosity must outrank cynicism in the pursuit of truth. His latest ventures in deep imaging and AI-driven diagnostics aim to redefine how we detect disease at the earliest stages, potentially saving countless lives. And beyond the laboratory, Nolan's foresight extends to the fate of humanity itself. He is an advisor on global security think tanks and engages with ideas of post-human intelligence, arguing that we must anticipate the ethical and societal challenges of technologies like artificial intelligence before they arrive.

Perhaps most striking is Nolan's willingness to explore phenomena at the edges of understanding – not to sensationalise them, but to glean insights that could propel us forwards. Whether examining a mysterious alloy from a reported UFO crash or scanning the brains of people claiming to have encountered the unexplained, he thoroughly scrutinises each data point. Nolan believes that even if 99.9% of such cases end up with mundane explanations, the remaining 0.1% could revolutionise our grasp of physics or biology. As he tells us in this conversation, Garry Nolan is steadfast in engineering the future by embracing the unconventional explanations for the unknown. His method – part inventor's workshop, part exploratory expedition – reflects a deep belief in human ingenuity. Nolan's ideas challenge us to broaden our perspective on innovation, knowledge, and even consciousness.

Please try your best to give us a snapshot of what you do?

I'm a tinkerer, and I develop technologies. Usually, I look for what is inevitable, and I try to visualise the inevitable. The idea is you reverse engineer the future, build a path towards it, and ignore the critics who say it won't work. You spend two years doing that, and then suddenly you make it, and everybody wants it. That's how I co-developed something called CyTOF. Another person at the University of Toronto invented the instrument, but our lab showed how it would be used to revolutionise immunology. We grouped up with the inventor of the proof of concept instrument, made a company out of it and sold it for over $200 million. The value was that it could do a deeper dive on the immune system, as opposed to previously where you could only look at a few markers that called out a few cell types at a time, say T cells or B cells. Now we could look at much of the immune system holistically and use algorithms to measure the statistical interplay and the dance of how the cells operate, one with another, and that dance tells you what the immune system is doing. It points to outcomes. We could, for instance, three months ahead of time, tell a woman that she has preeclampsia.

Then we developed two other instruments for doing it with biopsies (MIBI and CODEX), to look at the communities of cells and cancers. The idea was that we could look at the immune system and its interplay with the cancer but in the actual tissues themselves. It turned out that, just like in the blood, how the immune cells were positioned, and which ones were there and how close they were to which kind of tumour, predicted not only the outcome, but also told you where someone might develop new drugs to act on curing it.

How can we be better equipped to predict things happening in the future?

When AI first emerged, I saw it as an example of 'data off the curve'. I noticed people were engaging with something fascinating that most others were overlooking, so I felt compelled to understand how it worked. For me, data off the curve represents discovery. I often tell my students: when they present months of research, if something doesn't align, when most data points neatly follow a line except for one, we need to know why that one point didn't fit. Was it an instrument error? You can't disregard it. Your conclusions must explain all data points, not just the convenient ones. Each anomaly prompts me to pause – "Wait a second, go back a few slides" – because that's exactly where discovery lies. Predicting the future is one skill, but equally important is noticing when something is out of place and understanding its significance in how it predicts a future. Fortunately, I happen to be good at both.

How do you define your guiding principles?

I often get pushback on my ideas. The 293T cell retroviral production system is one of my most famous inventions. This brilliant scientist named Richard C. Mulligan invented a way to use retroviruses to move genes around, and I fell in love with it. But the problem was that it took three months to make them, and I happened to remember that I brought a cell line with me from Stanford. I was working in the laboratory of Nobel Prize winner David Baltimore. Richard had also gone through his lab and was already a professor at MIT. I brought the cell line that I remembered was highly transfectable, more so than any other cell line, meaning you could easily move DNA into it. I thought, rather than doing it Richard's way, if we did it this way, we could make viruses in three days rather than three months. And working with another postdoc in David's lab, we made it work.

I made a couple of cell lines when I returned to Stanford and made it easy for people to access. I was one of the first people on the internet to have my own lab website (back in the early 1990s). I had a link where people could download the material transfer agreement. I'd used many material transfer agreements before – they're five-page legal documents, what a mess and a hassle they are. So, I made a simple one pager: "You can use this, but you can't use it for any human purposes without permission. Just send us a FedEx number and we'll send it to you." I sent it to about 10,000 labs around the world.

I am commercially minded, and I have always noticed that first movers can blanket the marketplace before anybody, even if somebody has something slightly better. I got it out to thousands of labs, by which it became the standard. Every gene therapy done today with retroviruses, or lentiviruses, a kind of retrovirus, is done using the basic principle of the system I conceived. Every CRISPR experiment done in human cells, or even humans, that uses retroviruses is done with some variant of the 293T approach. It's had this enormous influence. But when I first said I would do it, and I told Richard, he said, "It won't work." Next to him, a Nobel Prize winner named Paul Berg sat there – they both knew me – and looked at me like "What are you talking about?" As an aside, I just won the Arthur Kornberg and Paul Berg Lifetime Achievement Award. I know Richard and Paul and Arthur were of exactly the same mindset. I was just like, "I'm not going to sit here and argue with you. I'm just going to go do it."

That's one of my guiding principles: don't wait for somebody else to permit you to do something you know is right. Don't wait for somebody to believe. Don't wait for somebody else to permit you to feel something should be studied if you think it's worth investigating. As much as those statements have worked for all my efforts in biomedical research, the same applies to UAP and UFOs.

Explain how this works concerning UFOs?

I didn't get into this because of some burning personal interest. I got into it because one day, while sitting in my office, the CIA knocked on my door and said, "We need to talk to you about some medical incidents." After verifying their credentials, I invited them in. They laid out an array of MRIs and CT scans, explaining, "These individuals claim they've been harmed by getting too close to certain objects." When I asked, "What objects?" their reply was cryptic: "That we'll tell you later."

This was around 2012–2013. I collaborated with them over the next few years. Very few cases involved individuals allegedly harmed by UFOs – initially, I thought it was a practical joke or a 'Candid Camera' moment. By 2015, we began referring to nearly all of the symptoms as 'interference syndrome', because these individuals appeared to be genuinely interfered with by external sources. We carefully correlated the diagnoses of the patients, grouped and classified, and found there was a pattern. When Havana syndrome emerged, it turned out our patient symptoms were so similar it merited transferring our findings and patients to a broader government analysis group.

After that transition, roughly ten individuals remained, and intriguingly, their accounts consistently included alleged interactions with aliens. By this point, I'd connected with other reputable government-affiliated scientists researching UFO phenomena. These were serious researchers – not jumping to conclusions, but speculating cautiously based on available data, including supposed reverse-engineering of crashed craft. Whenever I mentioned this work to colleagues at Stanford or elsewhere, the response was uniform concern: I was warned I could be ruining my career. That could not have been further from the truth.

If we're talking about a fifteen year window, firstly, how much closer do you think we'll be to a public understanding of literally answering the question: "We are not alone. We've proven it?" And secondly, how much would that actually impact society at large?

They're never going to prove the existence of extraterrestrial life by staring at a star 50 light-years away – or even eight or two light-years away – unless they literally see a tree growing there. Finding indirect evidence 50 light-years away would excite people, but mainly because it suggests such beings could already be here. It's easy and safe to speculate about distant stars, precisely because those claims can't be easily proven or disproven. But what if we took some of the funding we're dedicating to exploring distant worlds and redirected it towards investigating what's happening here, right now?

Consider the von Neumann probe concept: the universe is approximately fifteen billion years old. Even travelling at just 10,000 miles per hour, a probe could traverse our entire galaxy in about 500 million years. Such a probe could replicate itself, sending hundreds of copies across the galaxy – meaning it would take only half a billion years to essentially occupy the entire Milky Way. Given the universe's age, this could have already happened many times over. So, the argument that extraterrestrials 'can't get here' is absurd. Of course, they could be here. The real question is: are they?

It amazes me that I've found myself on Zoom calls or in meetings alongside four-star generals discussing these topics as established facts. I'm just a scientist – basically a fly on the wall – not the key person in the room. Sometimes I wonder if it's all just elaborate theatre, staged for my benefit – but who would bother, I'm not that important! But then again, I'm bound by secrecy agreements – I can acknowledge attending certain meetings, but I can't share specifics. What remains with me is what we scientists would call 'preliminary data'. Yet the more data I see, the harder it becomes to dismiss.

I've reached a stage in my career where I'm established as a creative thinker – someone who knows how to move ideas from lab to commercialisation – and I'm given more leeway than most. Publishing another paper on cancer might be professionally sound, but I'm already an author of hundreds of papers – exploring the reality of aliens is undeniably a more intriguing thing to do in the 'twilight' of my career. Thankfully, asking these questions hasn't hurt my career; if anything, it's enhanced it.

"Don't wait for somebody else to permit you to do something you know is right."

How so?   About five or six years ago, I engaged with the UFO community on Twitter ('UFO Twitter', as it was known then). Amid the endless arguments I saw ongoing, I advised people there to professionalise their approach – asking structured questions and using scientific rigour. I showed them how to counter debunkers effectively, and it had a significant impact on the following I created (I have over 100,000 followers at this point). But I also noted there were scientists like me eager to have serious conversations about this topic. That led directly to the founding of the SOL Foundation.

Recognising I needed a collaborator beyond the sciences, I partnered with Peter Skafish, an anthropologist and philosopher, as well as David Grusch, the whistleblower who testified under oath in front of Congress on alleged crash retrieval programmes. We created the SOL Foundation as a safe, structured space where scientists could openly discuss these phenomena without fear of ridicule. As soon as we established this platform, many previously hesitant people started coming forward. The truth is that people have always been interested, they've just been wary of the ridicule.

Today, at least five or six major scientific organisations actively engage with these questions. Initiatives now support commercial and military pilots in reporting anomalous experiences. A UK-based organisation called uNHIdden supports individuals claiming to have had 'interactive experiences', offering psychiatric support and creating spaces for group discussions.

In 2023, we held an unprecedented symposium at Stanford. Surprisingly, Stanford endorsed it – they even wanted their branding attached, something I didn't initially expect. Attendance was capped at two hundred due to capacity constraints, but the overwhelming response was relief and excitement: "Finally, I can openly discuss this with other normal, serious people."

Last November, a subsequent gathering in San Francisco drew around five hundred participants, and our next event is scheduled for Italy. Our primary goal is to normalise scientific and scholarly discourse on this topic, encouraging rigorous papers published in peer-reviewed journals. We're building an ecosystem around scientifically sound methods for investigating and writing about these phenomena.

A perfect example of the impact we're having occurred recently when I posed a question on X: "Can you patent alien technology?" In patent law, you can't patent something that's already been invented. However, current human patent law specifically applies to human inventions, not extraterrestrial ones, opening intriguing new questions about intellectual property and discovery. I posted the tweet, and within an hour there were dozens, if not hundreds of lawyers who came into the discussion, who had nothing to do with UFOs, but they found the problem interesting. As lawyers do, they found all the loopholes of getting around it. That's the idea – to set up quandaries and thought experiments for people to say, "Okay, let's war-game out the possibilities of 'what if'?"

"Publishing another paper on cancer might be professionally sound, but ... exploring the reality of aliens is undeniably more intriguing."

Exactly. It's about the power of branding, normalising ideas, and building community. But could these phenomena simply be us, from 5,000 years in the future? Does that even make sense? And how do these theories shape your understanding of time? As a layman, help me grasp this.

We don't have time travel – at least not yet. Perhaps we simply haven't developed the right theories. Similarly, we don't have warp drive, but emerging theories now show how it might be achievable. Theories are essentially blueprints – architectures that engineers can eventually use to build actual technology. That's precisely how quantum computing came about; quantum physics was purely theoretical until someone figured out how to construct a practical quantum computer 'machine'.

Two intriguing ideas emerge here. One involves bending or stepping outside of space itself, essentially looping back to observe earlier states – like anthropologists travelling to remote Amazonian tribes who have never encountered modern technology. It's conceivable that future beings might similarly travel back to observe their primitive ancestors.

When I hear reports from individuals describing encounters with humanoid beings, as a geneticist and evolutionary biologist by training, I find it difficult to believe these beings originated on another planet. Humanoid form is far from the optimal evolutionary design. Extraterrestrials might just as plausibly resemble an intelligent octopus or even a vegetable.

This leaves us with a few possibilities. First, they could be future humans who've diversified into radically different forms, returning with motives and hierarchies far beyond our comprehension. Second, they might originate from a separate timeline, entirely disconnected from our own, travelling freely across unimaginable periods.

The third scenario resembles the von Neumann probe concept – self-replicating machines spreading across the galaxy, observing but not directly interfering. These probes, controlled by a superintelligent AI (vastly surpassing our current technology and which would consider our ideas of AI laughably primitive), might create intermediaries designed to interact with native species. Such intermediaries would resemble us enough to communicate yet remain distinct enough to be unmistakably alien. Again, just an idea. Not a fact.

Like a godlike AI? Exactly. These beings wouldn't represent what's truly in control – they'd simply be agents of an intelligence far beyond our understanding, as incomprehensible to us as our emerging AI is likely to become. This leads directly into the challenges we face with artificial intelligence. Very soon, we'll need to treat advanced AI as an alien form of intelligence. Once it reaches artificial superintelligence (ASI), it will effectively be alien.

Regarding future-shaping technologies, are there other areas you're particularly excited about – technologies that will significantly impact our lives in the next fifteen years?

Every scientific instrument I've developed has allowed us to explore biology at increasingly detailed levels within cells. However, we've always approached biology indirectly – like reaching into a box with mittens, trying to understand intricate structures by analogy or inference. My approach now is: why not simply take the picture?

I've secured funding and started building an atomic imager that will achieve a resolution never reached before. Numerous experts have validated my idea, agreeing, "Yes, this will work – if you can build it." The challenge, of course, is that construction costs around $20 million.

How will this imager actually work, and what might it look like?

Here's a basic CAD drawing: it's essentially a vacuum chamber equipped with an ion gun, operating at roughly ten kelvin – extremely cold. While the technology itself isn't radically new, the innovation lies in significantly enhancing its capabilities. The core principle involves using an atomically sharp tip to pluck individual atoms off a sample by ionising them. With carefully placed differential plates – positive and negative – we extract these ions via quantum tunnelling. They strike the plates at precise points, revealing their original positions with about five-angstrom accuracy. While that's good, our goal is even greater precision – ideally sub-angstrom resolution.

Think of it like throwing a water balloon at someone behind you, knowing their approximate location but not exactly – you're aiming for pinpoint accuracy – you might splash them but it would be much more fun to hit them on the head! More importantly, we want to map atomic bond structures. The arrangement matters immensely: carbon atoms arranged one way create graphene; another arrangement forms diamond.

My innovation merges multiple methods to achieve far greater precision, allowing us to directly see atomic arrangements and bond structures. To manipulate matter as future civilisations will likely do – assembling technology beyond circuit boards – we'll need this atomic-level understanding. Alien technology, if it exists, would likely be configured in ways we can't yet imagine – like living cells, which aren't organised linearly but dynamically. My vision is to reach a point where we can programme matter itself into specific configurations – like embedding a reconfigurable supercomputer inside a baseball.

> "Very soon, we'll need to treat advanced AI as an alien form of intelligence. Once it reaches artificial superintelligence (ASI), it will effectively be alien."

Finally, where does this approach come from? Have you always been driven to challenge convention and confident enough to follow your own ideas? Your field is filled with hurdles – competing opinions, egos, and intense academic scrutiny. How did you develop this mindset that allows you to reflect on a remarkable career, while still enthusiastically pushing for new, groundbreaking ideas? What's your 'secret sauce'?

My 'secret sauce' is introversion – spending significant time deeply reflecting inside my own head. My husband frequently teases me for jumping straight to solutions whenever he presents a personal issue. He'll say, "Garry, I don't want solutions – I just want to talk."

From a young age, whenever I wanted something, I'd improvise it from whatever materials were available – baling wire, tape, anything to make it functional, even if imperfect. I was always drafting or making prototypes of things. Later, in high school and college, this translated into practical problem-solving in research labs.

Solutions often seem to simply appear in my mind. This phenomenon isn't unique; many scientists have described over the decades how posing a question clearly and then stepping away allows their subconscious to formulate an answer. It's the classic 'eureka moment' – ideas emerge spontaneously during routine activities, like walking or showering.

"Predicting the future is one skill, but equally important is noticing when something is out of place and understanding its significance."

For me, the key is fully immersing myself in all relevant information, trusting that my subconscious will eventually assemble the pieces into a coherent solution. This mental process involves deep brain structures – the caudate putamen and basal ganglia – which integrate memories, emotions, and desires. These same brain regions enable subconscious spatial awareness, allowing effortless navigation through crowded rooms. Remarkably, I've participated in Harvard-led brain research and discovered that my own family exhibits notably high neural density in the caudate putamen, potentially enhancing this intuitive cognitive processing.

Ivy Ross

Ross reshaped Google's hardware design by introducing softer forms, warmer materials, and greater emotional sensitivity into everyday tech products. Drawing from a multi-disciplinary background, her approach ensures that advanced technology feels intuitive and human-centred – pointing towards a future where devices support our lives rather than complicate them.

CHIEF DESIGN OFFICER FOR CONSUMER DEVICES AT GOOGLE

Across a career spanning close to half a century, Ivy Ross has worked for some of the world's biggest and most dynamic brands, from Coach to Calvin Klein via Swatch and Mattel. Today she is the Chief Design Officer for Consumer Devices at Google, leading a team that is responsible for the company's hardware products, and which has won over two hundred and forty design awards globally.

Yet her career began a long way from the tech world. Having studied at the Syracuse University School of Design and then the Fashion Institute of Technology in New York (where she majored in Jewellery Design), Ross launched her own jewellery brand: Small Wonders. It was then, as a jeweller, that she initially made a name for herself. She was, for instance, one of the first designers to use unusual metals such as tantalum and niobium in jewellery, metals which display an array of colours when charged with electricity. By the time she was just twenty-six, Ross had pieces included in the permanent collections of museums around the world, including the Smithsonian in Washington, D.C., the V&A in London, and the Cooper-Hewitt in New York.

As her pioneering use of materials as a jeweller showcases, Ross has always had an ability to marry beauty with forward-looking innovation. Today, she's doing just that at one of the biggest companies in the world. While she initially joined Google in 2014 to lead the second edition of Google Glass, the brand's augmented reality 'smart glasses', that product was discontinued the following year and Ross took over and grew the Design discipline for the entire consumer hardware area. She has since helped to transform Google, placing design firmly at its core. Under her leadership in 2018, the company launched its first installation at Milan Design Week. That same year, Google was recognised by Fast Company as the 'Best Design Company'.

A large part of her role today is imagining the future. As she tells us in this conversation, hardware products often take two to three years to bring to market, so Ross and her team are in a constant race to stay ahead of the curve. However, this has less to do with keeping up to date with the very latest technology releases; instead it's about trying to understand the cultural and societal shifts that might impact how we live and interact with technology in the future.

In the end, though, Ross believes that technology is fundamentally 'an enabler'. If it's designed well, it will more often than not enhance and improve our lives. Which is clearly why Ross tells us that she takes her job as a designer "more seriously than ever right now".

You've worked across a broad range of different fields, from jewellery design and fashion to consumer technology. Professionally speaking, how do you define your guiding principles?

Curiosity is one. It's probably why I've gone into so many different areas, because I pay attention to what catches my interest and I go down a rabbit hole of exploring. Craftsmanship is the second principle. I started out as a metalsmith, a maker. There's something beautiful about the connection between having an idea and being able to execute it with your own hands. So, no matter what I do, it's about thoughtfulness and craftsmanship. The final principle is humanity. At the end of the day, all of design is really about designing for people, for humans.

Let's focus on craftsmanship for a moment. I'm interested in your approach to materials, given your background as a metalsmith. You were one of the first jewellery designers to use titanium and other metals. How important is thinking about materials to your work today at Google?

My dad worked for the famous industrial designer Raymond Loewy, so the house I grew up in was always filled with interesting materials. Even when I was a baby, crawling around in his office, it was a very tactile experience. Materials have always inspired me, and I have always loved pushing and exploring the boundaries of materials. But right now, especially because of sustainability, design and materials are critical. I think the future will increasingly see designers working alongside scientists in new fields such as bioengineering to solve some of these problems together. At Google, for instance, we were one of the first companies to create fabric out of recycled plastic bottles, and we're constantly looking for ways to solve the biggest problems of our time. I feel it's a designer's responsibility.

"I think the future will increasingly see designers working alongside scientists in new fields such as bio-engineering to solve some of these problems together."

You mentioned that Google has used textiles made from plastic bottles. When it comes to sustainability, what areas are you and your team focusing on currently?

For electronics, sustainability and repairability are both big issues. We're very focused on exploring how we design things that last longer, but with electronics, there is the reality that certain things will have to be replaced. ==We're paying a lot of attention to the design details that will allow consumers to replace their own parts.== It's a huge difference for designers. It used to be all about working with our engineering partners to figure out how we can fit everything we want into a finite space. But once we'd worked that out and closed the door, we didn't have to worry about it. Now we want to understand how the owner can open it up easily themselves and replace a battery or a part. It's a fascinating challenge.

We're also working with our manufacturing partners on this. The only way we're going to change the industry is if we push the part manufacturers by demanding certain things, because otherwise they just keep making what they make. I've always advocated for competitors joining forces to push an industry in the right direction by putting pressure on that industry to invent new solutions.

For you, what's 'the next big thing' in the consumer-electronics industry, and how might it impact our lives?

Since the industrial revolution, humans have been optimising for efficiency and productivity, while putting some of the creativity, the imagination, the poetic nature of life, and the arts to one side as a nice-to-have, not a must-have. Artificial intelligence has been with us for quite a while, but now it's being amped up. It begs the question: what does it mean to be human? I see technology as an enabler and a tool – it's all about how you use it. I'm excited about these technologies taking certain rational things off our plates, giving us more time to invest in what it means to be human.

If I understand you correctly, are you saying that there's a part of humanity that can and will never be replaced by AI, and that it is something deeply creative?

Yes. I think we each take in information from the world and put it through our own filter that is totally unique to us. A machine can reference all the information in the world, but we have a unique filter. I love this quote by Jill Bolte Taylor (American author and neuroscientist): "Many of us think of ourselves as thinking creatures that feel, but biologically we are feeling creatures that think." We need to move into that feeling sense that only we can do and that is innate in us. If there's something that might do some of our thinking better, it pushes us back to being closer to our innate nature.

That's a really nice and positive vision of the AI-powered future that we're entering. How does that make you feel, particularly as someone who is working very deeply with AI and thinking about how it might change our lives?

I don't feel fearful or threatened. It's like any other technology or new invention. Again, I believe that design is about solving problems. We have this opportunity to look at how we take this technology and really make it useful to you. What can it do for you in your life that you're willing to surrender, which can unlock other things for you? It's inspiring a new thought process. I take my job more seriously than ever right now, because of the potential impact that these new technological tools might have.

"We're going to be looking at things from different angles, so there won't be this separation between architects, product designers, and experience designers. In the future, you might need to be all of these things."

> "Artificial intelligence has been with us for quite a while, but now it's being amped up. It begs the question: what does it mean to be human? I see technology as an enabler and a tool – it's all about how you use it."

Let's talk about how we as consumers will interact with our devices in the future. You joined Google just over a decade ago to work on augmented reality glasses, but when that division was closed down, you stepped into a role leading the company's hardware division. Few people have thought as much as you have about how we relate to the devices in our lives. How do you think this might evolve over the next, say, ten to fifteen years?

When we started the hardware division at Google ten years ago, our design aesthetic was about how we design technology so that it blends into the environment and doesn't stand out. But I can see a time when the physical hardware goes away altogether, because the magic will be embedded in our world. I might be talking myself out of a job here, but I think in fifteen years we might be there, insofar as you might not even need objects to initiate some of this technology. It might be a very fluid exchange of magic.

Is there a product you've worked on that shows Google's hardware moving in this direction already?

If you look at our new thermostat, it actually looks like a watch case. It's a beautiful domed glass piece. It doesn't look like technology at all. As you walk towards it, though, because of its sensors, it reveals the temperature inside. It reacts to you and gives you information when you need it, but not until such time. It's very magical. Even the visuals are beautiful – if there's a storm outside, it will show you a beautiful thunder line. ==For me, the future is not just about the object, it's the user experience and the object together, and making it magical.== It's about how the human affects the technology and how the technology affects the human. So it's a reciprocal act, a dance, more than ever before.

How do you think designers are going to need to adapt in order to help create this world that you're envisaging?

I think designers are going to get much more multidisciplinary. In the old days, you had to pick a swim lane, but I think we'll see more designers who have studied biology and science, for instance. We're going to be looking at things from different angles, so there won't be this separation between architects, product designers, and experience designers. In the future, you might need to be all of these things.

Take us inside some of the conversations you're having right now with your team at Google around creating products for the future. What are you preoccupied with at the moment?

There are such vast differences, when you think about the younger generations, they will have grown up in this world with another level of technology. We have to put ourselves in their shoes and try to fast-forward, to understand that they're going to have a different level of comfort with some of these things that are just coming online now. What does that look like, and how do we think about that as we advance in the future? Because in electronics, it takes two or even three years to build something – it's not like fashion, where it might take six months. You have to be even more considered, deep diving into the psychologies of these different groups, who they might be and what they might be thinking. We're dealing with very different groups and generations that have very different experiences, entering into a world that will be different too.

And that's presumably before you even take into account the fact that your audience, your customers, are all over the world. That must be another massive challenge?

Oh yeah! As our brand of electronics grows, even something like finding the right colour palette is challenging. When a Japanese customer buys electronics, it's often a sign of maturity and they want more neutral colours; yet certain groups in the United States want very different colours. How do you find a commonality and satisfy both? In the 1950s, there was one Eames chair that was the go-to chair. Now there are so many differences. I love that people are getting more individualised and finding their own expression. But the challenge for us is, how do you create the correct range of products without watering them down to find the commonality?

Let's take a step back and speak more generally. Aside from what we've discussed already, what creative or technological opportunities are you particularly excited about?

I've studied sound and vibration as a hobby for forty years. Alternative health has always been an interest of mine and I think we're entering a world where there will be a greater understanding of vibrational medicine and the power of sound and music. I'm looking forward to watching that world unfold.

Finally, thinking about how you and your team at Google work, is there any piece of advice you'd like to share with other designers out there?

We're always super inspired by nature. The universe is the best designer there is, so whenever I'm stuck, I look at how it creates. We always look towards nature for what we can learn from it.

"The universe is the best designer there is, so whenever I'm stuck, I look at how it creates. We always look towards nature for what we can learn from it."

Stefan Sagmeister

FOUNDER OF SAGMEISTER INC.

Sagmeister is one of the most influential graphic designers of the past fifty years. Known for iconic album covers, public installations, and exhibitions on beauty, he cleverly uses design to shift an audience's emotion and perspective. His work blends optimism, craft, and humour – proving good design can genuinely create joy.

Austrian-born, New York-based designer Stefan Sagmeister speaks to us from his sabbatical in Madrid. After all, this is a man with deep respect for time – and his every-seven-years sabbaticals are part of his methodical and personally precious creative process. His appreciation for time comes across in his latest book, *Now is Better*. Here, Sagmeister looks at the present day using data from the past to paint an altogether positive perception of how we are currently enjoying existence in the best time to be alive. This all relates to his philosophy that we need to take a more zoomed-out view of time, in order to tell us that the future will be better based on what we perceive from the past. After all, life expectancy has risen significantly over the past one hundred years, as has the number of the world's democratic nations.

Sagmeister's informed views come from seeing and doing much over a long and prestigious career. He first received international acclaim designing album covers for legendary musicians, including the Rolling Stones, Lou Reed, and Talking Heads. These works were more than decorative containers for the music inside; they were cultural commentary pieces, visual essays inviting deeper engagement with the albums.

From the 1990s until today, this innovative approach to visual storytelling continues. Sagmeister's portfolio combines projects that compel audiences to reflect, feel, and reconsider their perspectives. In 1993, he founded his studio, Sagmeister Inc., which later became Sagmeister & Walsh, expanding his repertoire into branding, installations, film, and immersive experiences. In recent years, he's downsized his studio to a headcount that enables close collaboration and a more intentional – hands-on – approach to their internationally celebrated design work.

This personal approach to craft, emotional intelligence, and hopeful foresight makes him an ideal figure for inclusion in *Ahead of Time*. His philosophy that design should 'help' and 'delight' resonates across disciplines. Moreover, his optimistic yet clear-eyed perspective on technology, sustainability, and cultural longevity provides valuable insight into how creativity can shape and enrich our collective future.

In the following conversation, Sagmeister explores these themes candidly. He discusses why, despite current setbacks, he firmly believes democracy and social progress will rebound stronger, how AI's impact will ultimately reveal human ingenuity at its best, and why tactile, haptic experiences will always hold enduring appeal. Most importantly, he tells us that cultivating short-term clarity and long-term perspective is critical in navigating our future.

From what I understand, in your recent book Now is Better, *you took a lot of data points and information, and then you were able to use it as a storytelling tool in a creative way to prove your thesis. With this in mind, are we generally looking at a better world in fifteen years' time?*

Yes, I believe so. **I'd rather be alive now than twenty years ago, and twenty years ago, I would have rather been alive then than hundred years prior, and hundred years prior, and so on.** Right now, democracy is going a step back, but we've been going two steps forwards for a long time. So, the absolute all-time peak of democracy was about ten years ago, and I'm convinced that, after this business with Trump, we will move forwards again as we've seen in the past.

In 1880, global warming was not measurable, but it was already on its way because the Industrial Revolution put an incredible amount of CO_2 into the atmosphere. When it comes to global warming, of course, we'll have to work incredibly hard to get rid of it. But, looking at the past, humanity has always been quite flexible in finding remedies for these adverse side effects so that progress could evolve again. And so I'm hopeful that we will again see these side effects.

What creative opportunities will the future present, and what role will technology play here?

AI will produce an incredible amount of terrible side effects. Still, I am optimistic even about something as unpredictable as AI. With this in mind, my stance on it comes from previous technologies. My go-to is the invention of the hammer. It turned out that more people built houses with hammers than killed their neighbours. So I believe in the good of people, and I think that, of course, there will be terrible actors that use AI in awful ways, no doubt about it. However, the ones who use it positively will outnumber and outlast the other guys.

"My go-to is the invention of the hammer. It turned out that more people built houses with hammers than killed their neighbours. So I believe in the good of people."

For you, what's 'the next big thing' in your industry, and how might it impact our lives? How does it make you feel?

Within our profession, the technology that everybody's talking about and everybody's afraid of, and some people are super excited about, would be AI. Three years ago, I would have said virtual reality. My partner has been working for the foremost virtual reality company that's created the best products. That company, which was pretty small, was bought by Meta, and it's not as exciting anymore as it used to be. However, I exercise using VR, and I think it works well, but I have not seen a single exciting product other than this three-year-old fitness product I'm using, so that progress seems to have stalled.

However, in my case, I'm excited to be involved with very haptic things again.

What creative opportunities will the haptic world present? What role does technology play here?

Haptic things that have been around for a long time have a good chance of lasting long into the future. I just read a scientific report about longevity, and they concluded that figuring out how long something will last is challenging. They said the best rule of thumb they could come up with is to check how long it has already survived. That was a reassuring note for me because we can use eighteenth-century painting – which is long-lasting – and put new inserts into it through our creative work, and we know it will last for another three hundred years. And if somebody wants to revise that creative work and make it contemporary again for the year 2300, they can be my guest and rework it.

It's funny. I know many digital workers that are now drawn to working with ceramics or porcelain to create things with their hands again. I see this trend among many people who started out working solely digitally. Digital work doesn't have an endpoint because any website or anything you're doing for social media or virtual reality never has an endpoint. There is something inherently unsatisfactory there. There is a reason why furniture makers seem to be at the top of the satisfaction chain when you look at professions ordered by happiness: when you're finishing a chair, you can see what you have done. And there is some sort of warm feeling when you're finished with it, you can look at it, you can sit on it, and it's a thing, and I'm sure that Benoît feels very similar when he creates a new version of one of his Ressence watches.

"Haptic things that have been around for a long time have a good chance of lasting long into the future."

How do you see the future in something like media? You're famous for your album cover artwork – but today, many of us only see them on a tiny phone screen.

If I look at Brooklyn, everybody is making their own marmalade, cooking fine dinners, and possibly enrolled on a ceramics course. When it comes to records – the vinyl world is tiny, but it's a very high-quality world. So for somebody like myself, who used to design many album covers, it's satisfactory because now people are appreciating the quality of the packaging, and the quality of the vinyl pressing is very high, higher than it's been during the last years of the original vinyl movement.

I buy a lot of those new vinyls because of their beauty. For $30 you can buy a fantastic piece of art and the vinyl. There is no other medium where you can buy an excellent piece of art for that price. If you go to a gallery you can't even get the catalogue for that price.

What other mediums of old media will survive? Bookshops are surviving and are doing very, very well. The best of the best of old media will survive.

If you put all your money on one aspect of life that you were confident about – say in fifteen years' time, we will still live like this – what would it be?

My crystal ball says that predicting the future, other than the long-term future, is not easy. I'm confident that people will still wear mechanical watches. I don't see that going away anytime soon because they already survived the smartwatch onslaught and the quartz crisis, and the love for something purely mechanical will always remain. There will likely be a small collector base who will take care of and love their petrol-driven cars, and it will probably be the same for vinyl. You will have a much smaller niche that loves cars, and the quality of these cars will be very high. I doubt that many people will love and repair their Toyota Corollas. It will be the same for watches. I have no doubt, and I can confidently say, that I will love and care for my Ressence watch.

"I'm confident that people will still wear mechanical watches. I don't see that going away anytime soon because they already survived the smartwatch onslaught and the quartz crisis, and the love for something purely mechanical will always remain."

How do you define your guiding principles?

I love to make work that helps and delights people. This is true for anything I call good design. And the helping aspect of these principles, of course, would be the functionality part of it. ==In the case of a watch, the helpful part is that it's readable and tells the time, and the delightful part is that it's just a pleasure to have it on.== And in the case of Ressence, it is that pleasure of how these discs interact with one another and how ingenious that system is, how pretty the watch itself is, how it has some sort of personality trait that I would like to have myself or maybe that I can identify with.

In my work, it could be something like the tunnels we designed that connect hospitals in Toronto. There, the functionality would be that you could wheel a patient through, feeling safe, because, in the past, children were terrified to go down into the basement. After all, the tunnels looked so scary. We created a new floor and designed the walls very colourfully, bringing back images of nature. We did a lot of research in that field and found that what works best as images of nature within the hospital environment. We could transform fear into delight. If a child is being accompanied through the journey, the nurse can say, "Look for all the bluebirds on the wall", "Let's count the bluebirds", etc.

Regarding AI, what creative/technological opportunities does the future hold?

Many of these AI digital artworks are so unoriginal. You saw the same when Photoshop was first introduced, where everybody did the same stuff. They will go in a similar direction with AI. I don't know. AI is not Photoshop, it's much more sophisticated. The possibilities are broader, significantly wider.

Stefan Sagmeister

Tell us more about your philosophy on time.

The statement 'the world is terrible' is accurate, and 'the world is fantastic' is true. The difference between those two statements is the time frame I look through. Now, if I look at today's X feed, or today's *New York Times* front page, every single item on it would be negative. And at the same time, if I widen the viewpoint, if I add three hundred years to my time frame, every one of those views on 2025 would be positive. From that point of view, it elevates the importance of a time frame.

Do you encourage people to take a wider-scope view of thinking about time?

One hundred per cent. We need both perspectives. Having the short-term view that social and traditional media give us every second, minute, and hour is essential. But having a long-term perspective is equally crucial, otherwise we risk giving up. There was a major study last year involving 100,000 young people, where 54% believed the world was ending. Those young people aren't actively fighting climate change or species extinction; instead, they're anxious and depressed, stuck in their bedrooms doing nothing to address the very problems they fear. ==Maintaining this broader perspective is essential: it helps us recognise how much better things have become in most areas that truly matter.==

"We need both perspectives. Having the short-term view that social and traditional media give us every second, minute, and hour is essential. But having a long-term perspective is equally crucial, otherwise we risk giving up."

One fact that always impresses me is that in mid-nineteenth-century France, the average daily calorie intake was about the same as Rwanda's in the 1960s when Rwanda was the most malnourished country. Back then, if you lived in France, you weren't concerned about global issues or who the president was, you just wondered how to avoid going hungry. Most people worked extremely hard yet only consumed about 1650 calories per day, far too little, living in conditions the UN would classify today as extreme poverty. Meanwhile, the remaining 10% – the king and nobility – held all the wealth and power. Sometimes, it's simply important to remember this.

Phil Schiller

APPLE FELLOW

Phil Schiller spent decades shaping Apple's brand, driving iconic product launches like the iPhone and the App Store. Now an Apple Fellow, his insights into product storytelling, user trust, and technology's social impact position him as a key voice, guiding how future tech innovations can balance commercial success and responsible design.

Phil Schiller has had a front-row seat to the evolution of personal technology. A three-decade Apple veteran and now an Apple Fellow, Schiller played a significant role in launching the products that defined the twenty-first-century digital age – from the iPod to the iPhone to the App Store and beyond. His tenure at Apple, which began in the late 1980s, saw him help shape not just devices but the very way we interact with technology in daily life.

Renowned for his passion for detail and talent for storytelling as a marketing executive, Schiller became Apple's chief showman on the keynote stage. Working closely with Steve Jobs through Apple's renaissance in the late 1990s and early 2000s, he mastered the art of blending technology and narrative to captivate audiences. This art remains massively copied by brands in the tech sphere and beyond up until today. Whether demonstrating a new iPhone feature or unveiling an App Store milestone, Schiller conveyed a contagious excitement for innovation. Equally important, behind the scenes, he fostered a culture of sweating the small stuff while dreaming big.

After decades of breakneck progress as a key player in the world's first trillion-dollar company, Schiller maintains a grounded perspective on where tech is headed. He's seen how impossible it is to predict the next big thing, recalling, for instance, how even insiders couldn't fully envision the internet's impact just a few years before it changed the world. For him, that unpredictability is a thrill rather than a worry, which means there's always room to create the future. In Schiller's view, humans shape technology's trajectory through curiosity and bold ideas – a reminder that people, not just processors, drive innovation.

Today, Schiller's eyes are on what's coming around the corner. He is optimistic about emerging fields like augmented reality and artificial intelligence, but also believes in responsible innovation. At Apple, he championed user privacy and simplicity and now brings the same insightful conscience to discussions of a better, safer future for AI. This makes Schiller's perspective a fascinating blend of optimism and realism – and a natural fit for Ahead of Time's look at future-shaping leadership.

While researching this interview, I watched a film of you at Apple's Worldwide Developers Conference in 2007. In it, you talk to Steve Jobs in the same way we speak today on a video call. You were showcasing groundbreaking tools at the time, which are tools that went on to change how we all live and communicate. Based on your career, how do you perceive time in relation to technology?

I think about it at several different levels. At the most straightforward level, I've learned that no one can truly predict the future. I have a simple example of that thought. In the mid-90s, we were working on things for usually three to five years out. Five years out, the internet was about to take off for consumers and businesses. And nobody back then predicted how huge its impact would be.

Indeed, people knew there would be some kind of network, a connected experience for us, but nobody knew what the internet was and what it would become. And if we can't see the most considerable thing coming less than five years away, that says our predictive powers aren't that super. There's nothing wrong with that. It's very exciting to accept that you don't know whether the things you're predicting and planning will be the future or not.

The result of accepting that you don't know the future means you need to be nimble and quick, and you need to be very observant of what's happening, and you don't accept that everyone says this or that is the future. Who knows? I enjoy living in a world where nobody's so super smart that they know everything that's going to happen, and ==the future isn't written in stone, and we can therefore create the future.==

Phil Schiller

There was a great computer scientist who worked for a bit at Apple, Alan Kay, who once said the best way to predict the future is to invent it. It becomes self-fulfilling. We don't know what the future will be, and we can influence it, and we can make a different bet than others are going to make, and maybe we'll be correct, and we can pivot faster than others can and respond quicker.

Professionally speaking, how do you define your guiding principles?

My biggest guiding methodology at work is passion. That's just how I'm wired. I love things I work on and devote time to, and I similarly like to work with people who share those passions, or have different passions, but they're passionate about something. I can connect with that and relate to that. So passion is number one, but second, it's simple, hard work, and the details matter. There aren't enough hours to refine something, so use every minute we can. You're never done. You just always keep working on the details. The things I've worked on, that others appreciate when they get into something, open a box, and take out a product – the box is beautiful, the product is beautiful, the instructions are beautiful, the font selection is beautiful, and the colours are beautiful. This effort shows that somebody cared about this when they made it. No detail is too small and no job is too unimportant to do to live up to delivering something wonderful.

A third point for me is that I'm very vocal. I speak up. Things get better through discussion, debate, and argument. I've always wanted to work in an environment where I can be vocal and collaborate with people who are vocal too. As long as we're all expressing different opinions for the good of the customer or the product, it's not ego-based. We all have the same goal, coming at it from various directions.

Another big one is admitting mistakes. I try to do that a lot with the team that I work with – be the first to say, "Hey, look, I screwed up, I made a mistake, and here's what I've learned from it, and here's why we will try a different path next time." You don't want to be the person who sweeps things under the rug and hides things. ==There's an old business saying that we learn more from our failures than our successes. But that's hard to do in practice.== Human nature is not to want to say I screwed up, but I try to create a culture where it is great to say I screwed up, as long as you learn from it and you move on.

I also encourage a working environment where we believe in checking your egos at the door. It's a job. We're working for somebody, we're working for our customer, we're working for our shareholders, we're working for the company. So everything we do has got to be about trying to live up to those expectations that others have, because that's so great when you can meet them and deliver on them.

And lastly, I will try to remember why I got into this. I came to Apple because I loved the products. I was amazed by them. I loved them, and every day, I try to remember and keep in touch with excitement about these products and technologies and what they can do, and I try to think about others who share that feeling and work for that. It's how I started, and I never want to lose that.

> "It's very exciting to accept that you don't know whether the things you're predicting and planning will be the future or not."

For you, what's 'the next big thing' in your industry/field, and how might it impact our lives? How does it make you feel?

It is AI at the moment. I say 'at the moment' because, again, we can't predict the future, but it's already impacting the present. There are a lot of definitions of AI, but the latest version of it are these large language models, LLMs, and they are pretty remarkable. I can now communicate with an AI bot that will go and research something for me or help me hone the quality of something I'm working on. And that is a pretty enabling technology. It's remarkable, and it's easy to imagine that it will be one of the most significant transformations in our industry since the internet. And it builds on one another – doesn't go away. That's another sign to me that it probably will be very impactful, because it builds on the biggest thing that's happened in decades with the internet, and it takes it further.

That brings both excitement and concern. Everything has a duality to it. Everything has both good and bad sides. It has excellent uses that will be wonderful, and there are concerning uses that can cause harm. So you would hope that people would take the time not just to rush things out, but to try to consider the consequences of the technologies and mitigate as many of them as possible, to make sure they're designed in a way that helps and augments humans' capabilities to do good work – not take away jobs, not have bad outcomes.

"We're already seeing the beginning of a new generation of language translation tools, based on AI models. It's the *Star Trek* 'Universal Translator' made real."

What other creative/technological opportunities does the future hold? What are you particularly excited about?

I have a passion for things related to the environment. That's something that is of personal interest to me. I wish I had answered your last question by saying, "the next big thing is the environment", I think that would have been wonderful. But in my industry, I don't believe that is the case. It's AI. So to your point, I would hope that we can use these technologies and these advances to help us in other areas, like the environment.

Imagine the ability to ask an intelligent assistant how you can complete a task or project in a way that's more environmentally friendly and has a better outcome. That is an example of how many potential good uses of this technology can augment our knowledge and our experience by connecting troves of information that we otherwise weren't even aware of to inform us of how to do something better.

Working with AI can, in some ways, be seen as working with a tool that improves efficiency. For example, Photoshop was a tool when it first came out – it was an industry-changing tool, but it was still a tool. How do you feel about that?

100%, there's no question that it is a tool. It's up to us to use these tools in responsible ways. It's up to us to know where they help and where they hinder. Those who use the tools best will benefit the most. With AI, these tools will be essential in any field. So it's about how to use them, not if you use them.

Here's another example – communication. We're already seeing the beginning of a new generation of real-time language translation tools based on AI models. It's the *Star Trek* 'Universal Translator' made real. The ability to comfortably travel the world and know what any sign says, or speak to someone you need to, will become a reality. Hopefully, this doesn't mean we stop learning new languages, but I think that kind of technological leap can be really powerful and beneficial to people.

Are you personally amazed by this time warp? In five years, I could probably wear an earpiece or glasses, and I could go to China and talk to people on the street.

It's funny. These things have been discussed for a long time, but they were eternally twenty-five years away. And then all of a sudden, boom, here it is, we're just about there. We're a single digit number of years away from some of these things that seemed like they were never getting closer for a while. It's fun. For example, things that are still forever in front of us, flying cars – that's probably still another twenty-five years away – but an earpiece or glasses that can auto-translate for you? That's hopefully coming in our lifetime. That's pretty exciting.

Thank you for such a far-reaching conversation. Is there anything else we've missed?

I'll share a quote that I love, which relates to much of this conversation. It's from Friedrich Schiller, the philosopher, "Art is the daughter of freedom." It's so profound. The idea that freedom gives rise to art, and then art helps us develop as people. It speaks to the importance of providing the freedom to explore. Are we creating, both in society and in our workplaces, that freedom to be creative and explore, which will give rise to art that challenges us or makes us feel fantastic? If you don't have that freedom, then you can't explore all the artistic expressions and outcomes that will help us develop wonderful new things. I believe it connects back to time and our current culture. Do we have enough freedom for that artistic expression?

Does this define the company culture at a place like Apple? How do you view this freedom to create and be artistic in the corporate world?

It's that challenge we discussed earlier on, that balance, that in the rush to get things done, one of the things people often give up is the time to have a complete exploration process. ==You want to ensure you're willing to create time and space for people to develop and explore new ideas.== Trying to find that balance. Things have to get done. Deadlines are wonderful things, as they are forcing functions to get things done, so you need those, but still, you want to make sure you have enough time before that deadline for exploration to occur.

Steve used to call it 'the intersection of liberal arts and technology'. Liberal arts are about exploring ideas and creativity, valuing the process of understanding something and thinking about it before putting something out in the world.

==**"I'm a glass-half-full guy, and I believe the future is hopeful and great. We're progressing towards better and better things, but we still have to recognise when things aren't always their best, and that's a challenge to make them better."**==

Tom
Segura

Tom Segura

STAND-UP COMEDIAN AND WRITER

Segura is reshaping comedy with fearless experimentation and sharp, candid storytelling. Known for sold-out tours and Netflix hits like **Sledgehammer**, he continually embraces emerging technologies – from streaming specials to podcasting – despite industry anxieties around AI-generated content. His comedy underscores authenticity in an age of digital façades, defining what it means to be genuinely funny in a fast-evolving media landscape.

Tom Segura has built a career in entertainment by firmly backing himself while choosing to ride the tide rather than swim against it. As a stand-up comedian, bestselling author, and wildly popular podcast host, he's leaned into the unpredictable nature of the entertainment industry – not by resisting change, but by embracing it. From being an early beneficiary of Netflix's rise to turning his attention to podcasting when it was still a niche medium, Segura's creative instincts have always been matched by a pragmatic view of the business behind the laughs.

Segura's blend of comic irreverence, blunt honesty, and sharp foresight makes him a vital cultural voice in any conversation about the future. He's direct and unapologetic, knowing he can't please everyone and refusing to cater to performative sensitivities. Segura is part of an independently minded generation of artists who are not just outspoken performers but entrepreneurs, running their own tours, selling their own merchandise, producing their own content, and experimenting with emerging technologies to reach new audiences. He views his work as both a craft and a business. "Your business is your comedy", he says. "And if you reject the idea that you're running a business, you're going to fail."

Segura is under no illusions about the scale of change underway in entertainment. AI is already reshaping the landscape, and he's paying attention. While some in the industry are panicking, Segura is curious. He sees potential in AI – particularly in animation and personalisation – but makes it clear that human nuance, delivery, and intent still define comedy's edge. He's not here to fear the technology or worship it. He's here to test it.

How future-proof is the business of comedy and entertainment?

The big debate right now, and the dilemma for many people in this space, is that AI is undeniably here, and we're only in the early stages of it. It's going to get much, much better very soon. ==The capabilities of AI right now are unimaginable; what it will be like in five years is beyond our comprehension, but we know it will be unbelievable.==

So what people in our space are dealing with right now is the fact that you can't act like 'I'm just going to ignore it'. There are a lot of people in our space who say, "It's stepping in for humans in writing and in acting. So it's bad. I'm not going to associate with it." I think the real work of the moment is understanding its capabilities and trying to figure out how you can utilise it without losing the human touch of creation. There's nothing you can do other than figure out how to adapt to it, rather than going around it.

Some people in the entertainment space are saying, "AI will be so smart in a few years that it'll have the ability to clone me, my voice, and everything." Where do you draw the line there, and where do you think it gets interesting?

Yes, we're currently in an experimental phase. We're in a time when you ask, "How can I use this without compromising myself?" And we don't have the complete answer on that. This is the time to say, "Okay, I'm going to act like I'm doing a field piece from Tokyo and see if I can make it entertaining and fun without making people feel weird." Maybe it will work, because we can lean into a comedic tone, where people go, "This is fun. This is in your voice. It does feel like it's you." There's also a thing where people don't like being duped.

We already had computers doing animation things. As opposed to the hand-drawn stuff. So animation is a space where it's more acceptable. I want to experiment with that. However, the only way to determine where the line should be drawn is by trying things out.

"People are hungry for authenticity. They're tired of the performative nature of so much social interaction. I think we're going to see a real hunger for people who just say what they mean and mean what they say. It's going to be refreshing in a world where everyone's so calculated."

So in a way, your industry is constantly evolving, and this next phase is natural. Or is it more frightening when we're talking about faking human beings?

It's both. It is the natural evolution, and it's somewhat terrifying. And the pushback on it is expected and natural. It should be like that. This year, Timbaland, the music producer, announced that he's putting forth his first AI artist, and the backlash was nuts. People really flipped out. And their whole thing was like, "Why do that? When there are so many great artists you could be championing and doing this and that."

But I feel like his take was: "Look, that doesn't mean I'm not doing the other things. This is just something I'm experimenting with." I applaud him because it takes a lot of nerve, and he knew that the backlash was going to come from that. It's just interesting to see what happens, even if it's a huge failure. We needed someone to do that, right?

It's like in my world of joke writing, the way you figure out the funniest thing is by messing up, saying the wrong thing, and then you go, "Oh, that was the wrong angle, or that's too far, or I crossed the line", and then you pivot. So we do need people to take these big swings and go too far. This is how you do it.

And we won't see ChatGPT writing your jokes anytime soon?

No, I don't think so. There's such a nuance that happens with jokes. It's the fact that so much of joke telling relies on your intent, intonation, tone, what you do with your voice, and your facial expressions. There are so many nuanced layers to it that I don't think that would work yet. But again, we're in the 1.0 version of this shit.

Even in an industry as seemingly slow as entertainment, you've leaned into new technologies and mediums from the start of your career. How come, and why is this valuable?

Sometimes you just get lucky with timing. I happened to shoot my first special in 2013, just as streaming was starting to take off. Back then, my goal was being on traditional television, so getting turned down was a real gut punch. Netflix felt like a consolation prize – at the time, they had about forty million subscribers, tiny compared to more than three hundred million today. I didn't realise I was catching streaming at an early growth stage; that's just how things lined up.

Similarly, podcasting initially held zero interest for me. My friends kept pushing me, saying, "It can help sell tickets." After a year, I noticed that people were coming to my stand-up shows because of the podcast. Again, I had no idea that podcasts would become such a massive part of our lives, attracting billions in advertising.

The big lesson was to always say, "I'll take the leap. I'll try it." I tell young comics today that while current platforms are established, there's always something new coming, like AI right now. You can't dismiss new media and tech; at least learning about them is crucial.

> "I always say that every stand-up comedian is an entrepreneur. Your business is your comedy, and if you reject the idea that you're running a business, you're going to fail."

Professionally speaking, how would you define your guiding principles?

One of the things I embrace as a guiding principle in comedy is that you have to remember that you're doing things that you think are funny. The kiss of death in comedy is: I'll do this because this group likes this. And then what happens is, your comedy doesn't appeal to anyone. ==So it's better to have something that 50% of people love and 50% hate.== Then you're like, "Well, if I think it's funny, then I'm okay with all those people hating it."

You have to remember, you started out wanting to do comedy because you thought something was funny and you wanted to share it with people. That authenticity is everything. The moment you start calculating what people want to hear instead of what you genuinely find funny, you've lost the essence of what makes comedy work.

Comedy must be one of the loneliest professions, in a way, even though it's so public. You're backing yourself from day one, right? And that's quite an entrepreneurial mindset as well.

I always say that every stand-up comedian is an entrepreneur. Your business is your comedy, and if you reject the idea that you're running a business, you're going to fail. You have to consider ticket sales, merchandise management, and planning routing and touring. You need a support group. You need a good agent. These are all moving parts, but the product is still your creativity, and you are an entrepreneur.

Today, you can't just think, "I'm just going to think about my comedy, everything else will take care of itself." No, it won't. You still need to understand that there are revenue streams, taxes, commissions, and travel expenses – that type of mentality will help your business thrive. The romantic notion of the starving artist might be appealing, but it's not sustainable if you want longevity in this business.

What creative/ technological opportunities does the future hold? What are you particularly excited about?

We often hear stories about newer, state-of-the-art mass public transportation, and there have been discussions about high-speed underground tunnels. I know that, at least in the United States, they have just lifted the ban on supersonic air travel. There are a couple of companies that are trying to re-enter that space. I find aviation and everything related to it fascinating. It would be amazing if we could travel between cities, especially internationally, at a fraction of the time it currently takes. Obviously you want everything to be thoroughly tested and highly safe, but I think it's exciting that we could be travelling from New York to London in just three hours.

There's also this idea that, for stand-up comedy, technology would one day allow us to perform remotely. You can already achieve this with hologram technology, but I'm referring to a higher level. I'm talking about a situation where you could have the ability to perform in one place and have people in a room 1,000 miles away watching you, but not feel like they're just watching a screen – feel like you're in the room. I feel that as technology improves, the concept of doing this becomes increasingly exciting, where you can perform for an audience and somehow be on a screen, seeing another audience, and feel like they're a part of it.

> "It's going to be like being real is the biggest flex you could have, just being authentic and not worrying about perception."

You're in a profession where audience interaction is the most crucial element, right? I wonder how it could work.

That's the thing, the natural thing to feel is: well, okay, if I'm in this room and you're not in the same room, then no. I get that because, of course, we want live reactions. However, I'm not opposed to the idea of the experiment. I recall that during the pandemic, performances would sometimes be held in a room with the performer alone, and then people would join on Zoom, which wasn't ideal.

==In my mind, I'm envisioning a higher level of technology, something that makes us feel more connected.== Perhaps it's haptic feedback or advanced audio technology that simulates the energy of the room, or visual technology so immersive that you forget there's a screen between you and the audience. The goal would be to maintain that essential human connection that makes live comedy work.

Tom Segura

With improvements in technology and communication, have you noticed people changing? Have people become more closed off? Will we continue to head this way because we're so obsessed with our smartphones and technology?

There is a phenomenon where we are obsessed with our phones. It has taken us out of real-world interactions. I think one of the things that happens, though, is that human beings are so programmed for the need, the necessity of human connection, that some of those people are deprived of it and when you give them a human connection, you see them really flourish, right? They want it, but some of them are unaware of their own need for it, because they feel that this digital interaction is providing them with everything they need. It's just not.

So we will see some pivot in some way, but it's so hard because we're so dopamine-driven by these devices that it's difficult to break away. But human beings still crave human connection. It's fundamental to who we are.

Are we moving into a world where people are increasingly worried about saying the wrong thing?

First of all, you should fully accept that you can say whatever you want. Some people say, "You can't say anything anymore." It's like, yes, you can. You can say anything you want. What you can't do is dictate that everybody else has to react a certain way. They don't all have to tell you it's great.

Part of it now is simply being aware that someone doesn't like it. I always tell people that thirty–forty years ago, when you would say something wild, some people would be upset by it; it's just that you didn't know. There was no social media. Someone couldn't tweet at you – they'd have to write you a letter and put a stamp on it.

What I've discovered, just being in comedy clubs and performing, is that you realise there's a huge portion of the population that is dying to hear these things. They want people to go for big jokes. You can hear and feel the release when a comedian takes a big swing at a joke that is on the line, and the crowd is just like, "Oh!" They just love it.

Do you see a correction coming when it comes to this fear many people have around never saying the 'wrong' thing?

Certain people are so concerned with saying the right thing. For me, I'm not concerned. I don't worry about it. I find it mildly amusing, sometimes hilarious, sometimes upsetting, but for the most part, I just barrel through people like that. I really do. Because I just go, "What are you doing? Is this for you? I feel like this is for you. We're going to say the right words to help you clap for yourself and pat yourself on the back. You're wasting time, and you're wasting energy by putting so much into this bullshit. Just speak."

The pendulum is always swinging one way or the other, and I think we've gone through this phase of inauthentic nonsense, with people so concerned about how they're perceived that you can feel the swing coming. It's going to be like being real is the biggest flex you could have, just being authentic and not worrying about perception. And look, if you're a piece of shit when you're being real everyone will know exactly who you are.

People are hungry for authenticity. They're tired of the performative nature of so much social interaction. I think we're going to see a real hunger for people who just say what they mean and mean what they say. It's going to be refreshing in a world where everyone's so calculated.

AHEAD OF TIME
20 Leading Minds Shaping the Future

Concept & Curation
Ressence

Interviews & Texts
Nolan Giles & Matt Alagiah

Final Editing
William Thomas Loftie

Graphic Concept
Gringos Design

Typesetting
doublebill.design

D/2025/12.005/9
ISBN 9789460583919
NUR 401

© 2025 Luster Publishing, Antwerp and Ressence, Antwerp
lusterpublishing.com
info@lusterpublishing.com
ressencewatches.com
info@ressence.be

Printed in Italy

All rights reserved.
No part of this publication may be reproduced, stored in a retrieval system, or transmitted, in any form or by any means, without the prior written consent of the publisher. An exception is made for short excerpts, which may be cited for the sole purpose of reviews.